Heckler & Koch's Handguns

by
Duncan Long

Edited by Larry Combs

Desert Publications
El Dorado, AR 71731-1751 U. S. A.

Heckler & Koch's Handguns

© 1996 by Duncan Long

Published by Desert Publications
P.O. Box 1751
El Dorado, AR 71731-1751
501-862-2077

ISBN 0-87947-153-0
10 9 8 7 6 5 4 3 2 1
Printed in U. S. A.

Desert Publication is a division of
The DELTA GROUP, Ltd.
Direct all inquiries & orders to the above address.

Front Cover:
Photographs and use of the HK logo are courtesy of Heckler and Koch, Inc, Sterling, Virginia.

Acknowledgments

Thanks must go to the many fine people at Heckler & Koch, Inc., who've supplied me with sample guns, photos, manuals, and other materials to help keep me "up to speed" over the years. Among these folks, Jim Schatz, Steve Galloway, Jo-Anne Powers, Donna J. Dallackiesa, John Meloy, Wayne Weber, Joe Jones, and Trina May all worked together with above-and-beyond-the-call-of-duty assistance offered over the course of several years' time.

A thank you must also be given to the other companies listed in this book who supplied me with photos, information, and sample products for the researching and writing of this book.

I must also express my gratitude to Larry Combs for once more helping to keep food on our table through his generous advance and for again fancying up my manuscript. And of course my usual thanks must go to Maggie, Kristen, and Nicholas.

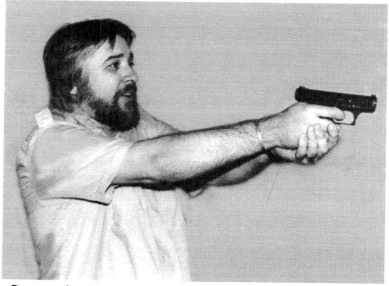

Duncan Long as photographed by his father Paul F. Long

Warning

Technical data presented here, particularly technical data on ammunition and the use, adjustment, and alteration of firearms, inevitably reflects the author's individual beliefs and experience with particular firearms, equipment, and components under specific circumstances which the reader can not duplicate exactly. The information in this book should therefore be used for guidance only and approached with great caution. Neither the author nor the publisher assumes any responsibility for the use or misuse of information contained in this book.

Contents

Chapter 1
Heckler & Koch

The company of Heckler & Koch as well as the locking mechanism employed on some of its pistols can be traced back to developments at the close of WWII when the German military was searching for a new rifle to help swing the tides of war back to the Germans' favor. Among the firearms being desperately developed was a new battle rifle developed by Haenel.

The military contract of 1938 was aimed at the creation of a rifle that would operate with the newly developed 7.92mm Kurz cartridge. Hugo Schmeisser headed the team that created the gas-operated rifle and, in mid-1942, had 50 prototypes ready for testing. The Walther plant paralleled Haenel's work with the development of a rifle for the new round; the Walther gun being based on the GA115, an earlier design they had created for possible military use.

The new guns were designated the MKb42 (or Machinen Karbiner– machine carbine–1942) with an "H" added to the designation of the Haenel weapons and a "W" for those of Walther. Nearly 8,000 of each of the guns were produced and tested extensively including in actual combat on the Russian front.

Heckler and Koch's Handguns

During the field trials the MKb42(H) proved to be superior to the Walther design. The rifle was modified by Schmeisser in 1943 with the inventor's modifications drawing from the combat experiences of the soldiers who had used the weapon. The end result being the "MP43" (Maschinen Pistole–machine pistol–1943) which was quickly adopted by the German military with the new weapon slated to replace the rifle, submachine gun, and light machine gun currently in use at the squad level by the Army.

The Erma, Haenel, and Mauser plants produced the rifles with subcontractors manufacturing some of the sub-components of the weapon (which had been designed to take advantage of steel stampings and simple wooden stocks). The MP43/1 was the first variant of the rifle; it had a screw-on grenade launcher rather than the clamping one originally designed for the rifle. The MP44 was the next version of the rifle (and–in the confusion of the war effort–is nearly identical to many of the MP43/1s though some lack the telescopic mounting bracket found on the MP43/1).

By 1944 the nomenclature of the rifle was changed; now it was the StG44 (Sturmgewehr–loosely translated "Assault Rifle"–1944). As the StG44 rifles were fielded in limited quantities, their concept proved to be quite effective, though the guns were quite heavy (weighing in at over 11 pounds unloaded). In an effort to produce a lighter rifle and save scarce resources, all the German manufacturers creating the rifles set out to create a lighter rifle modeled after the StG44 system.

The best of these was the Mauser GeratO6(H). This rifle employed a delayed blowback operation having locking rollers similar to the system used in the German MG42 machine gun; this system would later be modified and utilized in both the Heckler & Koch rifles and some of its pistols as well.

The new, easier-to-produce firearm came too late; the war was going against the Germans. Consequently, only a handful of the weapons were ever manufactured before the war came to an end. So the StG45(M) saw little, if any, combat.

In 1949, the German design team leaders that had worked on the StG45 formed a new company to manufacture precision machinery. Edmund Heckler, Theordor Koch, and Alexs Seidel set up their new business on the eastern slope of the Black Forest Mountains in Oberndorf, southern Germany. The new firm was became Heckler & Koch GmbH, Oberndorfam-Neckar.

Before long, Heckler & Koch created a prototype rifle which drew heavily from the earlier StG45 design the owners of the company had developed at the end of WWII. When Spain announced it was opening military trials for the selection of a new combat rifle, Heckler & Koch submitted their firearm, chambered for the larger 7.62mm NATO cartridge specified by Spain.

Heckler & Koch's new gun won the trials. The design of the rifle was modified to meet minor shortcomings displayed during the tests and a license to manufacture the gun sold to the Spanish government. This rifle was then manufactured in Spain as the CETME.

Following the acceptance of the first CETME design by Spain, West Germany started creating an army of its own (with Allied approval); it needed a new rifle to replace the M1 rifles loaned to them by the U. S. After a series of trials, Heckler & Koch's CETME Modelo 58s (designated the "G3") was selected as the best gun available.

In 1954, the German government asked for modifications to be made to the CETME design, retaining the "G3" designation for the new rifle. Once the changes were made, Heckler & Koch got a contract for the new German military rifle. Early guns were made in Spain and small numbers of the G3 were produced by the Rheinmetall plant in German under contract with Heckler & Koch. Later the production was handled by Heckler & Koch itself which produced the tooling to handle the military contracts. This gave the new company a base to fabricate and export G3s and soon other versions of the G3.

And soon the company was branching out to newly-designed pistols as well to reach the military, police, and civilian markets worldwide. In the mid-1960s the company introduced a submachine gun version of its G3 rifle. Chambered for the 9mm Luger, the "new" firearm was dubbed the MP5 (Machine Pistol Model 5). The gun soon became noted for its reliability and became popular in its various forms with special forces,

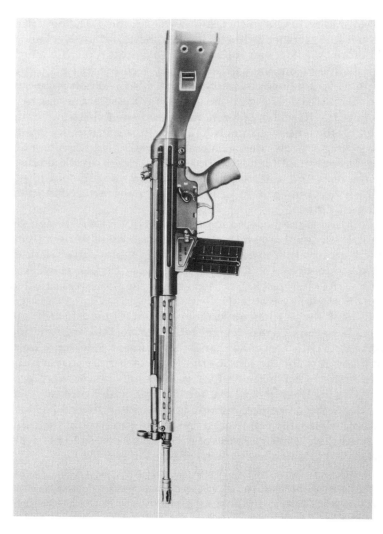

The G3A3 with fixed stock and "slimline" handguard. (Photo courtesy of Heckler & Koch, Inc.)

bodyguards, and other "pros" worldwide. Eventually a semiauto "chopped" version of the gun would even be marketed in the 1980s as a "pistol" (albeit a rather heavy "assault pistol" that, along with similar firearms, would soon bring down the wrath of the anti-gun movement in the U. S.).

Semiauto versions of the G3 rifles are popular in the U. S. SARCO imported semiauto versions of the G3 rifle into the U. S. for some time before Heckler & Koch decided to set up an operation of its own in America to cash in on the lucrative gun markets there. The new company was set up as "Heckler & Koch, Inc." in 1975 as a subsidiary of Heckler & Koch GmbH. The operation opened in 1976 at Arlington, VA. Three years later, the company relocated to new headquarters at Chantilly, VA; in the later 1980s, it made another migration to Sterling, VA.

While all pistols and rifles sold by the U. S.-based company were manufactured in Germany, the American representatives had an aggressive sales and training program aimed at U. S. police and military departments as well as civilian sales. This was bolstered by talented teachers and repairmen available to service weapons and train personnel who "bought into" the Heckler & Koch line. (For a more complete look at the various models of rifles and submachine guns developed by Heckler & Koch, see HK Assault Rifle Systems, available from Delta Press for $27.95.)

In a short time, Heckler & Koch firearms were not only popular with civilian shooters but also found in the hands of more and more police users, SWAT teams, and anti-terrorist squads. (Among the notable staff at Heckler & Koch, Inc., are John T. Meyer, Jr., a former Lieutenant in the U. S. Department of Defense Police where he served as a Special Reaction Team leader and Phil Singleton, who served six years in the Airborne and another six in the 22nd Special Air Services–SAS with tours in Northern Ireland, Central America, the Middle East, Southeast Asia–and the Falkland War. Such a staff wins quick approval of police and military personnel traveling to the Heckler & Koch, Inc., plant for training seminars.)

Heckler and Koch's Handguns

Since the manufacture of the first Heckler & Koch rifle was handled by CETME, the firearms became known as the "CETME" rifles. This is one of the first of the series "Modelo 58."

With the establishment of a "beachhead" in the lucrative U. S. market, Heckler & Koch, Inc. was soon expanding its market into both sporting and self-defense firearms. While the company's sporting rifles were never overly popular in the U. S., the company's military style semiauto versions of the G3 and MP5 were as were the various pistols the company imported into the U. S. from its parent company in Germany.

The first of the Heckler & Koch pistols to be seen in the U. S. was the P9S. This handgun had a double-action trigger system and was offered in both 9mm Luger and .45 ACP. With an eye both on defensive as well as the sporting markets, the P9S was offered in both a standard as well as a "Target" model.

As the German parent company and its subsidiaries grew, Heckler & Koch designers weren't allowed to rest on their laurels. Drawing from well-funded research programs, the company looked forward to a time when the G3 might become obsolete and set upon creating a weapons system for the 21st Century. With this in mind, company designers commenced work in the 1960s that led to the G11 rifle.

Heckler & Koch's work on an advanced rifle got an added boost in 1967 when NATO stated requirements for a caseless cartridge. At about the same time, the West German government started looking into the possibility of producing a sophisticated weapon that could "leapfrog" the .223 cartridge. This would allow the military to avoid having to switch to the smaller .223 cartridge and save a tidy sum in costs to boot since the G3 rifles were rugged enough to stay in service well into the 1990s or even the 21st Century until a suitable replacement could be created for the .223. So when the German government released their design specifications in 1970, Heckler & Koch had already laid much of the groundwork for producing such a rifle.

Caseless ammunition proved to be a tough nut to crack with most of the companies originally interested in the German and NATO call for a new weapon dropping out by 1973 leaving the field open to Heckler & Koch/Dynamite-Nobel. While the weapon the two companies worked on was still having problems with cook offs (ammunition firing spontaneously because

Heckler and Koch's Handguns

of the heat generated by rounds previously fired in the barrel), the two firms were confident the problem could be cured with new plastic coatings on the caseless cartridges.

The G11 rifle created by Heckler & Koch was designed to fit the caseless ammunition being developed for it, rather than—as is most often the practice modifying a standard rifle design and creating caseless ammunition for that. Heckler & Koch's basic design incorporates a "bullpup" layout (with the grip/trigger ahead of the receiver which lies inside the stock) in order to keep the length of a rifle within the specifications laid down by the German government.

At about this same time, the U. S. military started a search for a new rifle to replace its aging M16A2. So Heckler & Koch engineers revamped their G11 rifle slightly to conform to American specifications and entered another version of the caseless gun in the U. S. advanced combat rifle trials.

Despite the effectiveness of the G11 design, the end of the Cold War and general winding down of large military spending seem to have placed its adoption on hold both in Germany as well as the U. S. But many Heckler and Koch G3 rifles, as well as .223 and 9mm spin-offs, continue to be popular with police departments, civilians, anti-terrorist squads, as well as military users. (For a more complete look at the G11 and its development by Heckler & Koch, see Combat Rifles of the 21st Century, available from Delta Press for $19.95.)

In the pistol arena, Heckler & Koch designers got a boost in their development programs whenever governments started searching for a pistol to arm troops or policemen. Often these potential contracts for a new sidearm were accompanied by stringent requirements both for the durability of the gun as well as the basic layout of the firearm. Such "challenges" tested the abilities of Heckler & Koch engineers who always seemed to rise to the occasion, often with a gun unlike others the company had previously produced.

Perhaps the best known of these design endeavors took place under the Joint Services Small Arms Program (JSSAP) search for a new pistol.

G 11 RIFLE

GHGS

GESELLSCHAFT FÜR
HÜLSENLOSE GEWEHRSYSTEME

HK HECKLER & KOCH

Dynamit Nobel

Technical Data

Rifle

Caliber	4.73 MM ×33
Operating principle	Gas operated, firing from a closed breech
Breech system	Cylindrical drum
Bullet velocity -V₀-	Approx. 930 m/s
Modes of fire	Single fire 3 rounds burst Sustained fire
Rates of fire 3 rounds burst Sustained fire	>2000 rds/min. approx. 450 rds/min.
Magazine capacity	50 rounds

Dimensions:

Length of weapon	29.5 inch (750 mm)
Width of weapon	2.8 inch (71 mm) (partially 3.0 inch (77 mm)
Height of weapon	11.8 inch (300 mm)
Barrel length without chamber	21.3 inch (540 mm)

Weights

Weight of weapon with empty magazine	8.6 lbs (3.92 kg)
Weight of weapon with fully loaded magazine (50 rounds)	9.2 lbs (4.2 kg)

Round

Designation	4.73 MM ×33 DM 11
Total weight	80 grs. (5.2 g)
Bullet weight	49.2 grs. (3.2 g)
Total length	1.30 inch (33 mm)
Side length	0.31 inch (8 mm)
Reloading unit (Packaging) Capacity	10 rounds
Steelhelmet penetration	600 m

Optical sight

Magnification	1:1
Entry pupil	0.39 inch (10 mm)
Exit pupil	0.39 inch (10 mm)
Pupil clearance	1.37 inch (35 mm)
Field of view	200 mil
Eye piece adjustment	−0.5 dpt (constant)

G11 Rifle (Photo courtesy of Heckler & Koch, Inc.)

Heckler and Koch's Handguns

As the American involvement in the Vietnam War was winding down, the U. S. military did much soul-searching. One thrust of this rethinking was the realization that various branches of the service had not only adopted their own sidearms, many of them were even chambered for vastly different cartridges which created supply problems as well as maintenance nightmares for armorers.

The U. S. Air Force still had revolvers chambered for .38 Special cartridges for its fliers; the Army had the venerable 1911-A1 in .45 ACP; some special forces troops were armed with pistols that required 9mm Luger rounds; some target shooting was even being done with pistols chambered for the .22 LR or .22 Short. Throw in pressure from NATO to adopt a standard pistol cartridge and the military had some serious stocking and transportation problems when it came to getting arms and ammunition to the front during any battle.

Enter the JSSAP in the early 1970s.

This organization was created to "consolidate all small arms research, development, testing, and evaluation" according to government spokesmen. Instead of each of the five armed services picking weapons and ammunition willy nilly, there would be one central authority which would bring about cost savings and less confusion. At least that was the theory.

Unfortunately things didn't work out quite that way. Rather than start with just one weapons system at a time, the JSSAP staff decided to sweep the decks clear with a massive project that called for an entire family of firearms ranging from a new pistol through a new heavy machine gun.

Right from the outset the specifications of these weapons displayed oddities that one often sees when bureaucrats take command. For example, even though silenced weapons are rarely used by the majority of soldiers in the field, the JSSAP was intent on one standardized pistol. That meant the pistol was required to accept a silencer for those rare occasions when one was needed. This hamstrung things right from the start since a silenced weapon works best when it operates in a single-shot mode and has a fixed barrel — two features most modern pistol designs lack. Right out of the starting gate, the new

"XM9" pistol design requirements dictated features which would never be used on 98 percent of the pistols actually issued to troops.

As might be expected, critics and infighting between branches of the service brought much of the program to a standstill. The first round of tests finally took place at the Elgin Air Force Base late in 1981. At that point the Beretta 92SB appeared to be a clear winner of the tests.

But then Congress got into the act, apparently spurred on by gun companies in congressional districts. And Colt Firearms came up with a way to retrofit the old 1911-A1s in the government inventory to chamber the 9mm Luger cartridge — a substantial savings over buying new pistols. The JSSAP found itself pressured to conduct a second round of tests.

The second tests took place in mid-1982. The pistols submitted included the Smith & Wesson 459A, the Beretta 92SB, the SIG/Maremont P226, and Heckler & Koch's new P7 pistol. The results of this testing are unclear, but many insiders later claimed that Heckler & Koch's pistol won hands down.

Yet another round of tests were scheduled after Beretta and Smith & Wesson apparently threatened to sue the government over how the guns were tested.

After the third round, the dust and smoke cleared and this time Beretta came out on top once again with the SIG P226 now specified as an alternate choice of weapons, in part because it was more expensive but just as reliable as the Beretta 92SB. But many government agencies were less than pleased with the choices and were soon purchasing special pistols of their own. Before long, special units within the military were asking for their own choice of firearms rather than the generic "one size fits all" gun the JSSAP had selected.

By August, 1991, U. S. Special Operations Command ("USSOCOM" or "SOCOMM") awarded Heckler & Koch, Inc., and Colt's Manufacturing Company contracts to develop a "standard" pistol for the Air Force Special Operations Wing, the U. S. Rangers, the Navy SEALs, and the Green Berets, possibly with other U. S. law enforcement and anti-terrorist units. The guns had their basic requirements tailored to meet the spe-

Heckler and Koch's Handguns

cialized needs of these groups. Thus the XP9, originally adopted to supply both regular and special troops, now became the "issue" pistol for the regular troops.

Again Heckler & Koch took part in the trials. And, not satisfied in resting on past designs, the company developed a unique firearm that would soon be offered in a slightly altered configuration to the general public as well as eventually winning the trials to be adopted by the military.

The firearm specifications called for a weapons system that consisted of three components: A .45 ACP pistol, a laser aiming module (LAM), and a sound/flash suppresser (silencer). The program was divided into three parts. Phase I and Phase II were for the development and testing of the various weapons created while Phase III would consist of the actual production of issue weapons. The U. S. government would then decide whether or not to purchase pistols for issue to troops; if the go-ahead was given, the entire order would total 8,000 pistols and accessories. While this was hardly a huge sum, the added status of the company winning the contract as well as probable sales to other military and law enforcement users who would follow the USSOCOM lead promised to make it worth while.

A year after the announcement, Colt and Heckler & Koch delivered 30 prototype weapons for testing by the U. S. Navy. The testing was completed in March, 1993 and both companies give their best offers for costs of Phase II and III expenses.

On January 5, 1994, Heckler & Koch, Inc., announced that it had been awarded a "Phase II" contract to continue development of the USSOCOM's pistol, now known as the "Offensive Handgun Weapons System. At this same time the company was given a Phase III letter that offered a maximum of $15.8 million for the entire project (though the actual costs of Phase III were to be negotiated after Phase II development was completed). At this point the maximum number of pistols that would be purchased was reduced to 7,500, with full production slated to extend into April, 1997.

In July, 1995, Heckler & Koch announced the decision of the U. S. military to purchase its version of the USSOCOM pistol.

The company geared up for production of the pistols with the hope of added sales to other quarters as well.

Heckler & Koch pistols haven't always overcome the red tape and sometimes odd specifications required of guns submitted for military tests; but the company has continued to be popular with police, civilian, and military users worldwide. Like the company's rifles and submachine guns, its pistols have racked up good records by being both tough and reliable. This suggests that the company's firearms will continue to be popular on into the 21st Century.

Although Heckler & Koch GmbH has been acquired by the Royal Ordnance of Chorley, UK (which, itself, is a division of the British Aerospace Defense, Ltd.), the gun company continues to develop a variety of experimental firearms. And the design flair of the Heckler & Koch engineers promises that more innovative guns will be coming off the drawing boards and going into circulation worldwide. As the years pass, these firearms will continue to help soldiers, policemen, and citizens protect themselves when faced with danger.

Heckler and Koch's Handguns

Chapter 2
Pistol Models

The variety of pistol designs that have come from the Heckler & Koch factory almost defy belief. Most companies are satisfied to create one or two basic systems and then spin out various models through changes in barrel lengths, frame sizes, chamberings, etc. Not so with Heckler & Koch.

The company's engineers have developed everything from blow-back to roller-lock up systems for its handguns, each pistol showing distinct styling and design features unlike its sister firearms. Often these design features are even unlike those seen in any other company's firearms as well. This creativity continues to be apparent right up to the present time with the company's newest pistols.

HK4

The HK4 is a blow-back pistol that borrowed heavily from the classic Mauser HSc design of the 1930s with various refinements and different exterior lines. The pistol could be converted from one chambering to another with special "kits" offered for the handgun. Chambers/conversion kits included the .22 LR, .25 ACP, .32 ACP, and .380 ACP.

HK 4 (Photo courtesy of Heckler & Koch, Inc.)

During the 1960s, the pistol was imported into the U. S. and sold as the "Imperato HK-4". These guns were chambered in either the .380 ACP or .25 ACP. From the late 1960s through the early 1970s, the pistol was imported into the U. S. by Harrington & Richardson and marketed as that company's "HK 4" with models offered in .380 ACP and .22 LR.

When Heckler & Koch, Inc., was created, the pistol was imported by the new company as its "HK4" and offered with a set of barrels, magazines, and springs to quickly change from one of four chamberings to another. Eventually the gun was offered only in the .380 chambering with a .22 LR conversion as an optional accessory.

To accommodate the conversion from rimfire to centerfire, the shooter rotates a faceplate on the breech to adjust the impact point of the firing pin. An adjustable extractor makes ejection of spent cartridges reliable. These latter two refinements do away with the need to exchange the slide with cartridge conversions, greatly simplifying the changeover process and the expense of buying conversion kits. Conversion from one cartridge to another with the HK4 requires only an exchange of barrel, recoil spring, and magazine. This makes converting the pistol to another chambering quick and simple.

Specifications for the HK4

Caliber: .380 ACP (9mm Kurz), .32 ACP, .25 ACP, and/or .22 LR
Overall length of slide: 6.18 inches
Height: 4.33 inches
Standard magazine capacity: 7 rounds
Weight empty: 16.9 ounces

P7

The P7 was originally created for the Federal German Police and designated the "PSP" by Heckler & Koch. But the pistol is better known by the designation it got during the trials: The "P7" (Pistol number 7). Since its introduction, the gun has been modified to create a whole family of similar pistols and displays the ability of Heckler & Koch engineers to design firearms that are totally new in concept.

One of the basic departures from usual 9mm pistol design with the P7 can be seen readily in the lever that runs down the front strap of the pistol grip. This lever acts both as a safety as well as a cocking system for the striker and a slide release lever, giving shooters a firearm that is instantly ready to fire once it has been drawn and properly grasped. Additionally the design permits a light trigger pull similar to that found on more conventionally semiauto pistols employing a hammer. Should the pistol be dropped or otherwise released, the spring loaded lever on the front of the grip instantly returns to its safe position giving an added margin of safety to the firearm.

After the last shot has been fired in a P7, the slide remains locked back. This permits the empty magazine to be removed and a full magazine to be rapidly replaced. At this point, a simple squeeze of the cocking lever releases the slide, loading the pistol. Because the front lever acts as a safety, cocker, and slide release, there is little confusion for the novice shooter. When in doubt, he can simply squeeze the lever and be pretty sure he's done the right thing in preparing the pistol to fire.

Fifteen pounds of pressure on the safety lever is needed to cock the internal striker of the P7. Once cocked, the lever is held in place with just one pound of pressure, well within the normal grip pressure of most shooters.

After the safety has been engaged and the striker cocked, a light trigger pull fires the gun. For this reason, shooters must be very careful to keep the trigger finger out of the trigger guard until the gun is to be fired. Otherwise an accidental shooting is very likely to occur. Likewise care must be taken in selecting holsters since a tight holster pocket might place the safety in its "fire" position.

The trigger pull remains light throughout all shots fired from the P7; there's no shifting from a heavy to light pull as is the case with many double/single-action pistols. After firing the slide cycles to extract the empty brass and reloading a cartridge into the chamber; in the process the striker is recocked.

Original Heckler & Koch P7 pistol. Note lack of heat shield at top rear of finger guard (Photo courtesy of Heckler & Koch, Inc.)

Heckler & Koch's Handguns

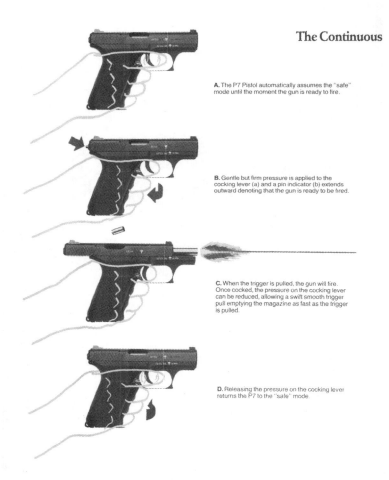

The Continuous

A. The P7 Pistol automatically assumes the "safe" mode until the moment the gun is ready to fire.

B. Gentle but firm pressure is applied to the cocking lever (a) and a pin indicator (b) extends outward denoting that the gun is ready to be fired.

C. When the trigger is pulled, the gun will fire. Once cocked, the pressure on the cocking lever can be reduced, allowing a swift smooth trigger pull emptying the magazine as fast as the trigger is pulled.

D. Releasing the pressure on the cocking lever returns the P7 to the "safe" mode.

Operation of HK P7 (Drawings courtesy of Heckler & Koch, Inc.)

Motion Principle

HK designed the P7 pistols for maximum efficiency with minimum trouble.

The "CONTINUOUS MOTION PRINCIPLE" is a result of years, dedicated to research and redesigning, to produce an *uncomplicated*, yet rapid firing pistol action that works with space-age precision.

The firing sequence of the P7 is simple: When cocking lever (A) is depressed; drag lever (B) is pressed back. Cocking latch (C) is engaged and holds drag lever (B) in place.

Transmission lever (G) is moved back at the same time as drag lever (B) and tensions firing pin (E) via compression spring (F).

When the trigger is pulled, the transmission (G) pivots sear lever (D) clear of cocking pawl on the firing pin (E) and at the same time, pulls down drop safety catch (H).

Under the action of spring (F), firing pin (E) accelerates forward and strikes primer cap in cartridge. Compression spring (F) returns firing pin to its rest position.

8 major components are involved in the firing process of the HK P7 pistol. An action like this is so simple, it's revolutionary!

Cutaway view of HKP7 showing front-strap safety and gas system. (Drawing courtesy of Heckler & Koch, Inc.)

Heckler & Koch's Handguns

Another departure from the norm with this pistol is found in its locking system. Rather than a levered delayed blow-back system, the P7 employs a delayed blow-back *gas* system similar to that found on many rifles. When the pistol is fired, hot gas is bled through a small port in the barrel into a chamber which then unlocks the slide after the bullet has left the barrel. This system permits a fixed barrel on the P7 which, in turn, translates to added potential accuracy of the firearm.

The P7's compact design coupled with a seven-round magazine makes it ideal for concealed carry, even though it has a full-sized grip. For this reason the P7 is often a favorite of undercover detectives or others wanting compactness coupled with the speed and accuracy of a semiauto action. And thanks to the safety lever and use of dual magazine release levers on either side of the grip behind the trigger guard, the P7 pistol is truly ambidextrous.

Muzzle velocity of the P7 is somewhat greater than with many other 9mm firearms thanks to a polygonal rifle bore. This design does away with the lands and grooves and instead achieves bullet spin through a spiraling dimensional twist inside the barrel. In addition to reducing fouling, the polygonal bore diminishes friction for a bit of added velocity to bullets.

About the only downside of the P7 has been its cost. The pistols have to be precisely machined and this translates into a higher price tag than is seen in other 9mm pistols. Nevertheless numerous shooters have opted for the P7 because of the unique features it offers.

Because of the gas system employed in these pistols, care needs to be taken in the selection of ammunition; cartridges that operate outside the normal pressure characteristics of factory 9mm Luger ammunition should, of course, be avoided. Most malfunctions are seen with cartridges that have been reloaded. With standard factory ammunition, the P7 and its sister guns are extremely reliable.

Since hot gas can cause lubricants to form a thick sludge, care must also be exercised when cleaning the P7. Obviously oil or other lubricants should never be placed or left in the gas system of this firearm.

Specifications for the P7

Caliber: 9mm x 19 Parabellum (Luger)
Overall length of slide: 6.54 inches
Height: 4.92 inches
Barrel length: 4.13 inches
Barrel rifling: Polygonal profile with right hand twist
Standard magazine capacity: 8 rounds
Weight empty: 28.9 ounces

P7 Target Model

Because the P7 fires with a fixed barrel having polygonal rifling, the potential accuracy is quite good. For this reason Heckler & Koch introduced a target model of the firearm, based on gunsmith Bruce Grey's design (and after whom the conversion pistol was named). These guns aren't cheap to make or purchase; consequently they're rarely seen at the range.

The Bruce Grey conversion sports an adjustable rear sight coupled with a raised front sight on the compensator. The compensator itself is fastened to the frame and extends 2.5 inches ahead of the slide. This compensator forms an expansion chamber ahead of the muzzle of the barrel; the gas is then diverted upward behind the bullet that exits the compensator.

In addition to the Bruce Grey/Heckler & Koch P7 Target pistol, several gunsmiths have created contest guns from the basic P7 pistol. Probably the best-known of these are the Pachmayr guns built by Les Pittman. These have a full-length slide extension welded to their front which is coupled with a standard-length barrel. Upon firing, gas is directed through the baffles and port of the slide to help reduce muzzle rise during rapid firing of the pistol.

A few gunsmiths have also altered standard P7s to contest configuration by rechambering the gun for the 9x21mm or .40 S&W cartridges. These cartridges offer an added edge in contests because of their greater power and/or width. However, since the P7 operates with a gas system, great care has to be exercised in such modifications of the pistol. Otherwise the

Heckler & Koch's Handguns

Heckler & Koch Target Model with Bruce Grey compensator. (Photo courtesy of Heckler & Koch, Inc.)

shooter is left with a firearm that malfunctions or operates in a manner that might become dangerous.

Specifications for the P7 Target (Bruce Grey)
Caliber: 9mm x 19 Parabellum (Luger)
Overall length of slide and compensator: 9 inches
Height: 4.92 inches
Barrel length: 4.13 inches
Barrel rifling: Polygonal profile with right hand twist
Standard magazine capacity: 8 rounds
Weight empty: 35 ounces

P7M7
This pistol is basically identical to the P7 but chambered for the .45 ACP. Unlike its sister gun, the P7M7 operates with a blow-back system with an oil-filled buffer that helps reduce recoil as well as wear and tear on the slide and shooter.

The P7M7 works well and the reduced recoil makes it one of the more pleasant .45 ACP pistols to fire, even though it is rather small when compared to most other handguns chambered in this round. Unfortunately the demand for a pistol this size chambered for .45 ACP is small. And the few shooters who want such a pistol generally opt for the more "traditional" guns based on the Colt 1911-A1. Therefore the P7M7 is no longer in production and the reintroduction of the pistol seems doubtful as well.

Specifications for the P7M7
Caliber: .45 ACP
Length of slide: 6.73 inches
Height: 5 inches
Barrel length: 4.13 inches
Barrel rifling: Polygonal profile with right hand twist
Standard magazine capacity: 7 rounds
Weight empty: 30 ounces

Heckler & Koch's Handguns

P7M8

The P7M8 is virtually identical to the P7. But with the introduction of the double-column P7M13 model of the pistol (see below), a new model designation for the original single-column P7 was needed. The only distinction between the P7 and the P7M8 is that the latter guns are probably a bit newer, having been made since the introduction of the P7M13.

In addition to its standard "blued" finish, the P7M8 is offered with a factory nickel finish. This transforms the pistol into a real "looker" that is also easy to clean and maintain.

Specifications for the P7M8
Caliber: 9mm x 19 Parabellum (Luger)
Overall length of slide: 6.73 inches
Height: 5 inches
Barrel length: 4.13 inches
Barrel rifling: Polygonal profile with right hand twist
Standard magazine capacity: 8 rounds
Weight empty: 29 ounces

P7M10

Although its model designation might suggest otherwise, the P7M10 was actually introduced after the P7M13. In fact, the P7M10 is basically the same pistol as the P7M13, but has been modified slightly to accommodate the popular .40 S&W.

Because of the large girth of the .40 S&W cartridge, the P7M10 holds only 10 cartridges in its double-column magazine. In addition to its standard "blued" finish, the P7M10 is also offered with a factory nickel finish.

Specifications for the P7M10
Caliber: .40 S&W
Overall length of slide: 6.73 inches
Height: 5 inches
Barrel length: 4.13 inches
Barrel rifling: Polygonal profile with right hand twist
Standard magazine capacity: 10 rounds
Weight empty: 30 ounces

Heckler & Koch P7M8 pistol (Photo courtesy of Heckler & Koch, Inc.)

Heckler & Koch P7M10 pistol. (Photo courtesy of Heckler & Koch, Inc.)

Heckler & Koch P7M10 pistol. (Photo courtesy of Heckler & Koch, Inc.)

Heckler & Koch's Handguns

Heckler & Koch P7M10 pistol / nickel finish.

Heckler & Koch P7M10 pistol.

(Photo courtesy of Heckler & Koch, Inc.)

P7M13

The P7M13 is basically the same as the P7/P7M8 but has a thicker grip to accommodate a double-column magazine. The magazine narrows at the top to cartridges into the chamber from the center. This permits use of the barrel, slide, and other parts of the original P7 in the newer pistol. The downside to this is slightly reduced magazine capacity as compared to what would be found if the magazine fed cartridges from the right and left positions into the chamber. However, given the compact size of the P7 design, this isn't seen as much of a handicap by most users of this gun. Too, it carries as many or more cartridges than most other "hide out" handguns.

Like its sister guns, in addition to its standard "blued" finish, the P7M10 is also offered with a factory nickel finish.

Specifications for the P7M13

Caliber: 9mm x 19 Parabellum (Luger)
Overall length of slide: 6.73 inches
Height: 5 inches
Barrel length: 4.13 inches
Barrel rifling: Polygonal profile with right hand twist
Standard magazine capacity: 13 rounds
Weight empty: 30 ounces

P7A13

The P7A13 was created for Military trials in the 1980s when the U. S. was looking for a new 9mm pistol to replace its aging 1911A1 .45 ACP pistols. The only notable departure from the P7A13 design is the slightly modified grip plates on the pistol. Otherwise the gun is nearly identical to the P7M13 pistol.

The U. S. military rejected the Heckler & Koch design for apparently unspecified reasons (though some who were involved in the testing claim the Heckler & Koch pistol won hands down). This is unfortunate since the compact size would have given the U. S. a single gun that could be used for a variety of purposes from a hideout pistol to a full-power, high-capacity sidearm.

Heckler & Koch's Handguns

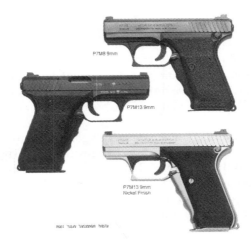

Three of the pistols from the P7 family. Top is the P7M8, center the P7M13, and on the bottom, the P7M13 with nickel finish. All three guns are chambered for the 9mm Luger. (Photo courtesy of Heckler & Koch, Inc.)

P7M13 (Photo courtesy of Heckler & Koch, Inc.)

P7M13 (Photo courtesy of Heckler & Koch, Inc.)

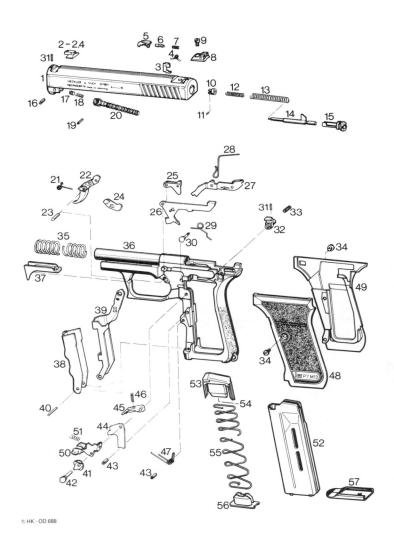

© HK - OD 688

Heckler & Koch P7M13 exploded diagram

Pistol Models

1	Slide	28	Sear spring
2	Front sight (height 6.4 mm)	29	Rocker spring
2.1	Front sight (height 6.6 mm)	30	Rocker spring axle
2.2	Front sight (height 6.8 mm)	31	2 x Front sight / slide retainer pin
2.3	Front sight (height 7.0 mm)	32	Slide retainer
2.4	Front sight (height 7.2 mm)	33	Slide retainer spring
3	Drop safety catch	34	2 x Grip screw
4	Drop safety catch spring	35	Recoil spring
5	Extractor	36	Receiver with barrel
6	Extractor spring guide	37	Cover for trigger guard
7	Extractor spring	38	Squeeze cocker
8	Rear sight	39	Drag lever
9	Rear sight screw	40	Squeeze cocker axle
10	Firing pin collar	41	Rocker
11	Firing pin collar pin	42	Magazin catch axle
12	Inertia spring	43	2 x Stop pin
13	Firing pin spring	44	Stop
14	Firing pin	45	Cocking latch
15	Firing pin bushing	46	Cocking latch spring
16	Piston pin	47	Squeeze Cocker spring
17	Piston detent	48	Grip, left
18	Piston detent spring	49	Grip, right
19	Piston retaining pin	50	Magazine catch
20	Piston	51	Magazine catch spring
21	Trigger spring	52	Magazine housing
22	Trigger	53	Follower
23	Trigger pin	54	Follower insert
24	Transmission lever	55	Follower spring
25	Disconnector	56	Locking plate
26	Slide catch lever	57	Magazine floor plate
27	Sear bar		

HECKLER & KOCH GMBH

D-7238 OBERNDORF/NECKAR

(Chart courtesy of Heckler & Koch, Inc.)

Heckler & Koch's Handguns

Heckler & Koch P7A13, created for US Army trials. (Photo courtesy of Heckler & Koch, Inc.)

Specifications for the P7A13

Caliber: 9mm x 19 Parabellum (Luger)
Overall length of slide: 6.73 inches
Height: 5 inches
Barrel length: 4.13 inches
Barrel rifling: Polygonal profile with right hand twist
Standard magazine capacity: 13 rounds
Weight empty: 30 ounces

P7K3

The P7K3 model is outwardly identical to the other P7 guns with several important distinctions: It has a non-fixed barrel and operates with straight blow-back, without a gas delay lockup; an oil-filled buffer helps decrease recoil and save wear and tear on the slide. The blow-back design permits chambering the pistol for lower-powered centerfire cartridges and also makes it practical to switch chamberings with a proper conversion kit.

Heckler & Koch P7 (bottom left) shown next to "hideout" pistols that are either "chopped" models of larger guns (like the 1911 variant at the lower right) or .380 pistols (like the top two pistols). The compact size of the P7 makes it ideal for a variety of missions.

Heckler & Koch's Handguns

Conversion kits include the .22 LR, .32 ACP, and .380 ACP. While the P7K3 is arguably a bit large for a hide-out gun in these lower-powered chamberings (especially given the fact that the P7M8 is the same size *and* chambered for the more potent 9mm Luger), those who shy away from recoil might prefer one of these chamberings. In terms of self defense, the .380 version would be the best bet.

P7K3 shown with conversion slide and barrel. (Photo courtesy of Heckler & Koch, Inc.)

The Heckler & Koch P7K3 with its adapter kit. (Photo courtesy of Heckler & Koch, Inc.)

A shooter having a .22 LR version of the P7K3 along with the .380 conversion kit or even a 9mm or .40 S&W version of the P7 might employ the P7K3 for practice. The lower noise produced by the .22 coupled with the reduced damage downrange makes it more ideal for practice in areas that might restrict shooting larger centerfire cartridges. There might also be a cost savings in practicing with a .22 pistol, though the high price tag of the P7K3 would dictate a lot of practice before such a savings could be realized.

Specifications for the P7K3

Caliber: .22 LR, .32 ACP, and/or .380 ACP
Overall length of slide: 6.73 inches
Height: 5 inches
Barrel length: 4.13 inches
Barrel rifling: Polygonal profile with right hand twist
Standard magazine capacity: 8 rounds
Weight empty: 29 ounces

P7PT8

The P7PT8 is a training pistol that fires a special, plastic-bullet cartridge designed for the gun. The handling and service operations of the pistol are identical to the standard P7M8, except for the fact that it won't chamber standard 9mm cartridges. In order to keep the pistol from being confused with a standard pistol, a large blue dot is found on either side of the front of the slide.

The slide on the P7PT8 is lighter than on the standard pistol and lacks a gas system, instead operating on a blow back system that employs a floating chamber to increase recoil force enough to activate the slide so the pistol can be fired in standard semiauto mode.

Because of the high initial velocity of the plastic bullets used in the P7PT8, it is capable of inflicting a lethal wound at close ranges. However the light weight of the bullet causes it to drop to the earth by the time it has traveled 125 to 170 meters. In addition to use as a training pistol, the operating characteristics of the plastic bullets make the gun ideal for some types of

Heckler & Koch's Handguns

Heckler & Koch P7PT8 (Photo courtesy of Heckler & Koch, Inc.)

anti-terrorist operations where a close-range weapon capable of inflicting wounds but incapable of doing damage at longer ranges is ideal. That said, it does not appear that this gun has been put to such use — though the tight-lipped tendencies of anti-terrorist teams may have kept actual use of the P7M8 in such circumstances secret.

Specifications for the P7PT8

Caliber: 9mm x 19 Parabellum (Luger)
Overall length of slide: 6.73 inches
Height: 5 inches
Barrel length: 4.13 inches
Barrel rifling: Polygonal profile with right hand twist
Standard magazine capacity: 8 rounds
Weight empty: 27 ounces

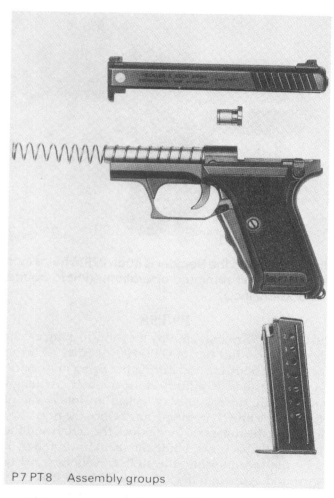

P 7 PT 8   Assembly groups

Disassembled Heckler & Koch P7PT8. Small part above the barrel is the floating chamber.   (Photo courtesy of Heckler & Koch, Inc.)

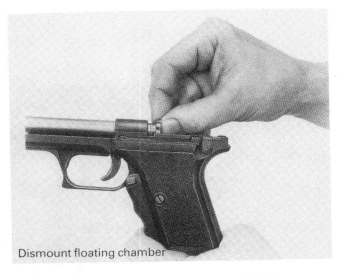

Dismount floating chamber

Floating chamber in the Heckler & Koch P7PT8 helps increase the recoil to permit semiauto operation. (Photo courtesy of Heckler & Koch, Inc.)

P9/P9S

The P9 and P9S pistols employ the same locking mechanism Heckler & Koch used for its G3 series of rifles. This system exploits the pressure created during the firing of a cartridge to push a pair of rollers to either side of the bolt. As long as the pressure is high, the rollers stay locked in slots in the pistol's slide to keep the breech from opening. Once the pressure drops to a safe level, the rollers no longer lock the action and the slide is then free to fly back, extracting the spent brass and then, propelled by the recoil spring, the slide travels forward to load another round. Although the P9S appears to be striker fired, in fact it has an internal hammer, enclosed by the slide. This dictates a thumb-operated hammer release which also acts as a slide release; this all-purpose lever is located on the left side of the grip plate (making it a bit less than ideal for left-handed shooters). Unfortunately the pistol also has an unhandy slide-mounted safety that's hard to disengage.

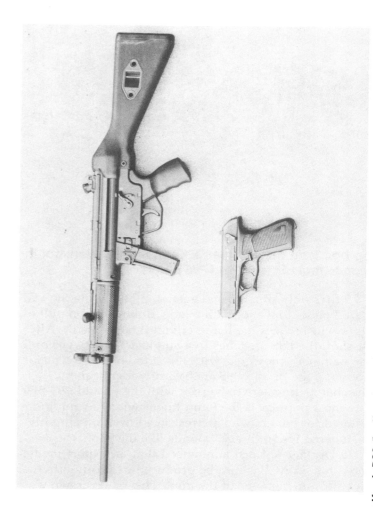

Heckler & Koch P9S (bottom) employs the same locking system of Heckler & Koch's rifles and carbines like the HK94 above it.

Heckler & Koch's Handguns

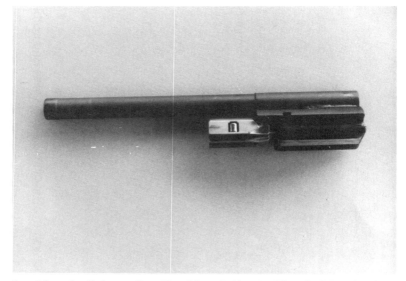

Locking bolt from the Heckler & Koch rifles is identical in operation to that of the P9 and P9S pistols.

The P9 fires only from a single-action mode while the P9S can be fired on its first shot with a long, double-action pull of the trigger which cocks the hammer and then drops it. After the first shot, the P9S switches to a single-action trigger pull until the hammer is lowered with the side lever. Except for this difference, the P9 and P9S are basically identical.

Three chamberings are to be seen with the P9 and P9S pistols. The most popular is the 9mm Luger with 7.65mm guns being offered for buyers who are restricted from owning firearms chambered for "military" rounds like the 9mm.

In 1975 Heckler & Koch announced that an export model chambered for .45 ACP would be produced in addition to the 9mm and 7.65mm versions of the gun. This new version was offered only in the P9S configuration and was apparently created with an eye toward U. S. sales.

Unfortunately for Heckler & Koch, this model was fielded just as large numbers of shooters in the U. S. were switching to

Heckler & Koch P9S (Photo courtesy of Heckler & Koch, Inc.)

Heckler & Koch's Handguns

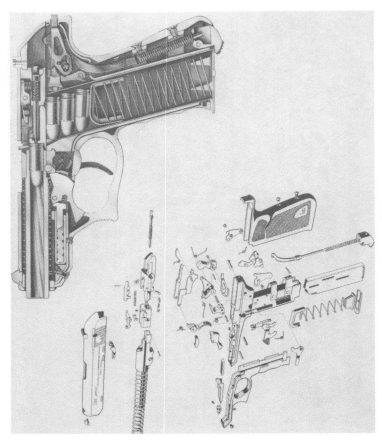

Cutaway and exploded views of Heckler & Koch P9S (Drawings courtesy of Heckler & Koch, Inc.)

The P9S Pistol

Schütze / shooter	Anschlagart / firingposition		Haltepunkt bei	Entfernung	25m
Herrmann	aufgelegt from rest	oder for Schießmaschine mashine rest	point of aim	distance	27,3yd
Bemerkung/remark	Datum/date	Datum/date 25 Jan 1984	Kaliber/caliber .45 ACP	Waffen-Nr./weapon no. 406 703	
Heckler & Koch GmbH Oberndorf / Neckar		Mod. P 9 S	Prüfer / inspector JM		

Heckler & Koch P9S, with its non-tilting barrel, roller locking system, and hammer-forged barrel offers superb accuracy. (Photo courtesy of Heckler & Koch, Inc.)

the 9mm cartridge. The .45 model is dimensionally a bit larger than its sister version, but overall nearly identical.

Like most other Heckler & Koch pistols, the P9 and P9S make use of a polygonal bore to increase muzzle velocity. The grip of the P9/P9S is basically a skeletal sheet metal assembly to which a polymer trigger guard/front strap is added. The pistol grip then encloses the sides and rear of the frame. Coupled with the use of many stamped parts, the overall cost of the pistol is therefore kept in check, despite the use of a machines (and arguably complicated) bolt and bolt carrier and roller locking system.

Early guns have a rounded trigger guard while later pistols produced from the late 1970s on display a recurved trigger guard. This permits the then-popular two-handed hold that placed the index finger of the off hand on the front of the guard for added stability.

The P9 and especially the P9S have proved popular, especially in Europe. However the complicated bolt assembly of this firearm has dictated that it has never been as popular as other more conventional pistols.

During the 1980s, U. S. Navy SEAL teams were said to have ordered specially configured P9 pistols for evaluation. According to some sources, these guns had the single-action P9 trigger assembly with a three-round burst option in addition to standard semiauto fire (this seems unlikely given the small magazine of the P9, but stranger requirements have been seen in government contracts). These 9mm guns are also said to have been equipped with high sights that permitted sighting the pistol when a silencer tube was mounted on the gun; it seems likely these guns have a threaded muzzle to permit attachment of silencers to the firearm.

Specifications for the P9/P9S (9mm and 7.62mm)
Caliber: 9mm x 19 Parabellum or 7.62mm
Overall length: 8.01 inches
Height: 5.38 inches
Barrel length: 4.06 inches
Barrel rifling: Polygonal profile with right hand twist

Standard magazine capacity: 9 rounds(9mm and 7.62mm)
Weight empty: 29.9 ounces

Specifications for the P9/P9S (.45 ACP)

Caliber: .45 ACP
Overall length: 8.01 inches
Height: 5.5 inches
Barrel length: 4.06 inches
Barrel rifling: Polygonal profile with right hand twist
Standard magazine capacity: 7 rounds
Weight empty: 32.5 ounces

P9S "Sport Competition"

This target version of the P9S took off where the basic pistol left off and was made only in a 9mm model. The P9S Sport Competition came standard with an adjustable rear sight and a trigger that could be adjusted both for its weight of pull as well as its over-travel. With the usual Germanic eye toward detail, the Target model was sold with a compact screwdriver that could be employed for adjusting the sight and trigger.

The Target model could be purchased with an optional 5.5-inch barrel with a weight-style compensator attached to its over-size barrel; in this configuration it is generally seen with the Heckler & Koch optional wooden grips. The grips came in two styles, one is a checkered "combat" grips similar to the plastic grips of the standard P9S while the other is stippled target grips which are "oversized" with thumb and palm rests.

The P9S Sport Competition was also offered in a "kit" form with a standard length barrel and slide as well as a long barrel with slide and compensator weight. This gun also came with wood and plastic grips making it possible for the owner to configure it in a variety of ways.

Specifications for the P9S Competition

Caliber: 9mm x 19 Parabellum or 7.62mm
Overall length: 7.56 inches (short barrel); 9 inches (long barrel)
Height: 5.5 inches

Heckler & Koch's Handguns

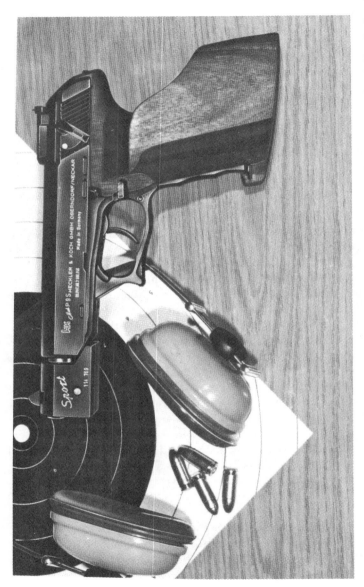

Early model of Heckler & Koch P9S Sport Competition (Photo courtesy of Heckler & Koch, Inc.)

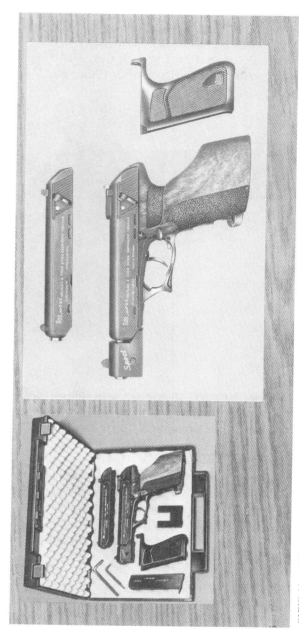

"Kit" Heckler & Koch P9S Sport Competition with spare barrel/slide assembly and grip along with wrenches needed to exchange parts on the gun. (Photo courtesy of Heckler & Koch, Inc.)

Barrel length: 4.06 inches or 5.5 inches
Barrel rifling: Polygonal profile with right hand twist
Standard magazine capacity: 9 rounds (9mm and 7.62mm)
Weight empty: 35 ounces

P9S Sports Competition Model

Late model Heckler & Koch P9S Sport Competition. Note front sight, lack of "Sport" engraving on compensator and "matte" finish. (Photo courtesy of Heckler & Koch, Inc.)

VP70 and VP70M

Although Glock pistols are often credited with being the first "plastic frame" handguns, in fact the little-heralded VP70 has this distinction. The VP70 frame is mostly high-strength polymer with steel reinforcement inserts and, like the later Glock that followed in its footsteps, also employs a double-action striker firing mechanism.

Unlike the "pre-cocked" striker on the Glock, the VP70 requires that the striker be cocked with the trigger before each shot. This makes for a very heavy pull that one writer likened to the pull of a staple gun. In fact the pull is not quite that bad;

the initial heavy pull for cocking the striker gives way to a lighter and crisp let off on most pistols. Once a shooter gets used to this pull, it can be accurate, with the inherent accuracy of the gun's fixed barrel undoubtedly helping out.

The VP70 has an impressive magazine which holds 18 rounds without extending beyond the grip of the pistol. The magazine release is located at the bottom, rear of the pistol grip.

The gun employs a non-locking system which utilizes a blow-back design that's rarely seen with the potent 9mm Luger that this pistol is chambered for. To make such a system work, a heavy recoil spring and slide are used with the VP70.

The sights on the firearm are unique and, unfortunately perhaps, have never been utilized on other pistols. The front sight has a notch cut down its center, creating a clear sight picture regardless of the lighting conditions.

The VP70 is large for a handgun. But there's an important reason for this. The pistol was designed to be employed either as a handgun or a machine pistol. True machine pistols (as opposed to carbine-like submachine guns which are also sometimes called "machine pistols") have never been overly successful.

The reason for this lack of success is that the locking mechanism of most pistols isn't suited to rapid automatic fire and the light weight of the guns generally means that a machine pistol's muzzle climbs rapidly during automatic fire. The first few rounds are at the point of aim but after that the gun is shooting at the sky. Additionally, the rapid cycling of the small slide on most pistols dictates that the magazine empties quickly even with the most careful of trigger control on the part of the shooter.

Designers of the VP70 attempted to get around all of these problems. First off, the pistol has a heavy slide and fires with a blow-back system. These features put the gun out front right from the start. Additionally, the VP70 can't be fired in the auto mode without the attachment of a special shoulder stock designed for the gun.

Only when the stock is attached does it become possible to fire the weapon in its burst mode by using the selector mounted at the top, front of the stock assembly. Placing the selector lever

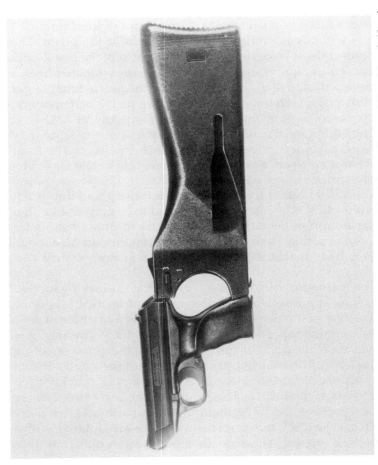

VP70M with selective-fire stock attached (Photo courtesy of Heckler & Koch, Inc.)

at "1" gives semiauto fire; the "3" gives a three-round burst with each trigger pull. The stock acts as a make-shift holster when the gun isn't attached to it; in theory at least, this makes carrying the stock less of a problem when it isn't attached to the pistol.

The pistol is designed to fire only in semiauto or, with the stock in place, with a three-round burst. This helps do away with the problem of a gun climbing off target and emptying its magazine in the process, even with the pistol's high cyclic rate of 2,200 rounds per minute.

The VP70 arguably does the best job of performing in the machine pistol mode of any handgun yet designed. However the stock connection is a little less than secure with the pistol "flopping" to each side a tad when attached to the stock. This doesn't bother the operation of the firearm, but is sometimes a bit disconcerting to users who expect a very tight lockup of the two parts.

Additionally, while the pistol functions well as a machine pistol, it comes close to actual submachine gun dimensions when the stock is attached. Consequently many potential buyers during the period the gun was available from Heckler & Koch undoubtedly opted to purchase Heckler & Koch's MP5 guns rather than go with a pistol/stock combination that had to be assembled to work and didn't have that positive of a feel to it once assembled.

Undoubtedly the real "death knell" came from the company's own designers. Working on creating a compact submachine gun, Heckler & Koch engineers took the MP5 to its smallest extreme, deleting the firearm's stock and cutting the barrel back to five inches. The new "MP5K" had a grip added ahead of the magazine well for additional stability and eventually trigger mechanisms that operated in a three-round burst mode were made available.

Heckler & Koch designers even created shoulder harness assemblies for concealed carry of the MP5K; additionally a hide-out briefcase and carrying bag were also created for the MP5K, permitting bodyguards to carry the gun discreetly while still being able to lay down massive amounts of fire in a moment's notice. When it's all said and done, the successful design work that created the MP5K undoubtedly led to the demise of the VP-70 as well as the machine pistols developed by other manufacturers during recent years. (For more about the MK5 and its variants, see *HK Assault Rifle Systems* available from Delta Press for $27.95.)

While early VP70s were known simply by that designation, with the development of a semiauto version of the gun aimed at the civilian market, the selective-fire model become the "VP70M" (Military) while the semiauto-only became the VP70Z (see below).

Specifications for the VP70/VP70M

Caliber: 9mm x 19 Parabellum (Luger)
Overall length (without stock): 8.03 inches
Overall length (with stock): 21.5 inches
Height (pistol) 5.38 inches
Barrel length: 4.57 inches
Barrel rifling: Six grooves with right hand twist
Standard magazine capacity: 18 rounds
Weight empty pistol (without stock): 1.7 lbs.
Weight empty (pistol with stock): 2.82 lbs.

VP70Z

The VP70Z is basically a semiauto-only version of the VP70. Although these guns had a small following in the U. S., sales were poor, undoubtedly because of the large size of the gun compared to other 9mm pistols on the market as well as its heavy 17-pound trigger pull. Too, the magazine release on the VP70Z was located on the base of the grip, a position favored in the past by Europeans but greatly disliked by most U. S. shooters or others interested in rapidly reloading a pistol in the middle of combat.

Although the double-action trigger of the VP70Z makes the need for a safety arguably unneeded, Heckler & Koch offered a safety as an option on the guns it marketed.

Specifications for the VP70Z

Caliber: 9mm x 19 Parabellum (Luger)
Overall length: 8.01 inches
Height: 5.38 inches
Barrel length: 4.57 inches
Barrel rifling: Six grooves with right hand twist
Standard magazine capacity: 18 rounds
Weight empty: 1.7 lbs.

SP89

The semiauto SP89 is nearly identical to the Heckler & Koch MP5K stockless version of the company's submachine gun. Although similar to a selective-fire weapon, the SP89 lacks the forward vertical grip on its handguard, apparently to meet with BATF approval. Since the forward grip is missing on this model, the gun sports a barrel extension about an inch long to help keep a shooter's fingers from straying in front of the muzzle.

Because the SP89 is built around the basic frame and pistol grip of the company's submachine gun, it accepts a wide variety of accessories made for the MP5 including 30-round magazine. The pistol also accepts many accessories designed for the G3 rifle, including target grips, scope mounts, etc., making the firearm an all-purpose "target pistol", self-defense, or just plain fun shooter.

Despite the fact that the SP89 was simply a 9mm pistol that happened to resemble a submachine gun, the anti-gunners in Washington, D. C., were soon out to ban it and similar firearms. Consequently the gun is no longer imported into the U. S. following the "Crime Control" act passed late in 1994. (For a closer look at the G3 rifles, the MP5K, and various accessories for these firearms, see *HK Assault Rifle Systems* available from Delta Press for $27.95.)

Specifications for the SP89

Caliber: 9mm x 19 Parabellum (Luger)
Overall length: 12.8 inches
Height: 8.26 inches

Heckler & Koch's Handguns

Right-side view of SP89. (Photo courtesy of Heckler & Koch, Inc.)

Left-side view of SP89. (Photo courtesy of Heckler & Koch, Inc.)

Heckler & Koch's Handguns

P89 with scope mount and target grip created for the company's G3 rifle. (Photo courtesy of Heckler & Koch, Inc.)

Width: 1.96 inches
Barrel length: 4.5 inches
Barrel rifling: Six grooves with right hand twist
Standard magazines capacity: 15 or 30 rounds
Weight empty: 4.4 lbs.

USP

The USP (Universal Self-loading Pistol) marked a new high for Heckler & Koch, Inc., because it was the first firearm to be more or less designed by U. S. engineers for the U. S. market and *then* developed in Germany. Where previous guns offered by Heckler & Koch, Inc., had been designed for worldwide government or police markets, the USP has the distinction of being created specifically for the U. S. civilian and police markets.

The original USP was introduced in 1993 and marketed in the new .40 S&W chambering with the 9mm Luger added shortly thereafter. 1995 saw the introduction of the .45 ACP model of the USP at the SHOT Show in Las Vegas, Nevada.

In order to meet the many different preferences of American shooters, the gun design permits modification of the safety and trigger to a variety of configurations without major alterations to the pistol's mechanism. This makes possible ten different configurations of the pistol in single-action/double-action as well as double-action-only models. Since the safety lever is "modular" in design, it's practical for an Heckler & Koch-trained armorer to quickly change the USP from one safety configuration to another. (When the gun is field stripped, most safeties are marked as to their configuration on the small "white" metal section normally covered by the slide.)

The frame-mounted safety lever is easily manipulated with the thumb and (in some versions) also acts as a hammer drop mechanism when depressed past the "fire" position. The lever can be reversed by an armorer for left- or right-hand use (though the lever isn't ambidextrous in itself).

The possible configurations currently offered by Heckler & Koch include:

The standard (Number 1) permits the "cocked and locked" style of the 1911-A1 with the hammer back and the safety

Heckler & Koch's Handguns

USP .40 S&W pistol. (Photo courtesy of Heckler & Koch, Inc.)

Left-side view of USP chambered for .45 Auto (Photo courtesy of Heckler & Koch, Inc.)

Right-side view of USP chambered for .45 Auto (Photo courtesy of Heckler & Koch, Inc.)

USP...the choice is in your hands.

Variant 1
Double Action/Single Action **with "safe"** position and control lever (manual safety/decocking lever) on **left** side of frame

Variant 2
Double Action/Single Action **with "safe"** position and control lever (manual safety/decocking lever) on **right** side of frame

Variant 3
Double Action/Single Action **without "safe"** position with control lever (decocking) on the **left** side of frame

Variant 4
Double Action/Single Action **without "safe"** position with control lever (decocking) on the **right** side of frame

Variant 5
Double Action Only **with "safe"** position and control lever (manual safety) on the **left** side of frame

Variant 6
Double Action Only **with "safe"** position and control lever (manual safety) on the **right** side of frame

Variant 7
Double Action Only **without control lever** (no safety/decocking lever)

Variant 9
DA/SA **with "safe"** position and control lever (manual safety/no decocking function) on the **left** side of frame

Variant 10
DA/SA **with "safe"** position and control lever (manual safety/no decocking function) on the **right** side of frame

There are currently nine different variants of the USP safety/trigger system. Variant number 8 is currently missing from the lineup. (Photo courtesy of Heckler & Koch, Inc.)

engaged; this version also permits safely lowering the hammer by depressing the safety lever. This version can also be carried with the hammer down, safety on or off, with first shot fired via a double-action, long trigger pull after which the gun reverts to single action mode with the hammer back after each shot.

The Number 2 safety variant is the left-handed version of the cocked-and-locked arrangement.

Number 3 deletes the manual safety mode so the lever acts only to lower (or decock) the hammer if the shooter isn't about to fire; the gun can be fired by pulling the trigger through its double-action pull after which the pistol fires from single action.

Version Number 4 is the left-handed version of number three with the lever on the right side of the frame.

Number 5 is the double-action-only configuration; each shot requires a long pull. The safety lever can be engaged or left in the fire position with this option.

Number 6 is the lefty variant of Number 5.

Version 7 is a double-action-only version lacking any safety.

Number 8 is not currently marketed by Heckler & Koch. According to insiders at the company, this designation was temporarily applied to a variant of the pistol tested by an unspecified government agency. In fact it appears that Version 8 was actually identical to Number 7 but had tritium night sights rather than the standard iron sights.

The Number 9 variant has a safety without hammer dropping so the pistol can be operated more or less like the 1911-A1 (making it ideal for contest shooters).

Number 10 is the left-handed variant of Number 9.

In addition to the manual safety found on some models of the USP, the pistol design has other safety features. These include a double-action hammer intercept notch, a firing pin block, and a disconnector. The hammer itself normally remains in a "rebound" position away from the rear of the firing pin. Only when the trigger is pulled back will the momentum of the hammer drop permit it striking the firing pin. Otherwise

Single control lever. Up for safe, down for fire, all the way down to decock

Multiple automatic and internal safeties

Control lever can be changed to opposite side for left hand shooters

Extended slide release

Shielded ambidextrous magazine release

Extra large trigger guard for use with gloved hands

Patent pending recoil reduction system lessens stress on the pistol and lowers the recoil impulse felt by the shooter

Universal mounting grooves in the frame allow for mounting lasers sights, scopes, or other accessories

Easy to field strip & maintain, a reliable & dependable pistol

USP pistol in its .40 S&W version with inserts showing various features of the firearm. (Photo courtesy of Heckler & Koch, Inc.)

67

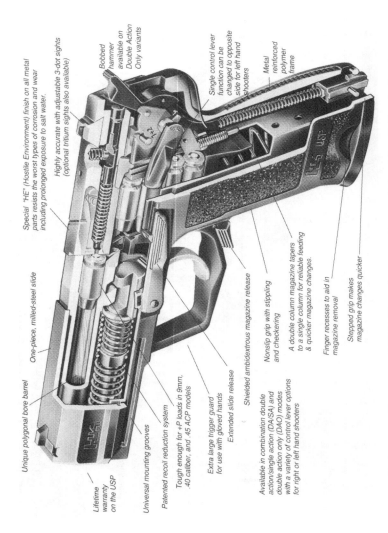

Special "HE" (Hostile Environment) finish on all metal parts resists the worst types of corrosion and wear including prolonged exposure to salt water.

Highly accurate with adjustable 3-dot sights (optional tritium sights also available)

Bobbed hammer available on Double Action Only variants

Single control lever function can be changed to opposite side for left hand shooters

Metal reinforced polymer frame

One-piece, milled-steel slide

Unique polygonal bore barrel

Lifetime warranty on the USP

Universal mounting grooves

Patented recoil reduction system

Tough enough for +P loads in 9mm, .40 caliber, and .45 ACP models

Extra large trigger guard for use with gloved hands

Extended slide release

Shielded ambidextrous magazine release

Available in combination double action/single action (DASA) and double action only (DAO) modes with a variety of control lever options for right or left hand shooters

Nonslip grip with stippling and checkering

A double column magazine tapers to a single column for reliable feeding & quicker magazine changes.

Finger recesses to aid in magazine removal

Stepped grip makes magazine changes quicker

Cutaway diagram of USP (Drawing courtesy of Heckler & Koch, Inc.)

the hammer cannot travel forward enough to reach the firing pin.

The hammer has a bobbed, upward pointing spur that ends in grooves for a secure thumb purchase if the shooter opts to thumb it back (on double/single-action models). While, in theory at least, this also permits safe lowering of the hammer by placing a thumb on it and pulling the trigger, there is always room for error with this maneuver. Consequently the hammer should always be dropped with the safety/hammer-drop lever to avoid any chance of an accidental firing.

The pistol utilizes many innovations that make the gun stronger and more durable than one might expect. Made of injection molded polymer reinforced with glass fibers, the frame has four steel inserts above the trigger and rear of the frame for added strength. The grip panels are molded into the frame and have a stippled finish for a more secure grip.

Realizing that a variety of accessories like laser sights, scope mounts, and other devices were becoming popular with American shooters, Heckler & Koch engineers decided to create a mounting system that would make adding such devices to the pistol much easier. To do this, the front of the frame was kept square and parallel to the sighting plane of the USP and a groove added to either side of the frame. This makes it easy to mount laser sights or small flashlights on the firearm, thereby making it suitable for illuminating or pinpointing a target. Heckler & Koch also offers a muzzle brake assembly for the USP which attaches to the frame, transforming the pistol into a target pistol for those needing such a gun. (These accessories will be covered in detail in subsequent chapters.)

The USP has also been designed for quick operation. Both the trigger guard and slide release are oversized to permit firing the pistol with gloves on as well as quick reloading of the USP. The rear sight is well designed and dovetailed into a slot in the slide; an optional tritium night sight is also offered by Heckler & Koch, Inc. The sight is non-adjustable, though Heckler & Koch offers replacement blades to adjust the height and drifting the sight to one side modifies the "windage". For added speed in aiming, the top of the slide has tapered edges, drawing the eye to the sights.

The barrel is, as one might expect from Heckler & Koch, hammer forged with a polygonal rifling. The modified locking system borrows from the Browning High Power. This linkless system was refined by Peters Stahl and is often found in target guns. In theory this system would also permit easy barrel exchanges for switching the chambering of the pistol from 9mm to .40 (or vice versa), though currently Heckler & Koch appears to have no plans for such conversion kits.

The recoil guide has a buffer spring riding inside the main spring on the recoil spring guide; acting during the last compression of the recoil spring, the heavy buffer spring reduces the last impact of the slide on the frame at the very rear of the recoil cycle. Heckler & Koch engineers claim that this buffer reduces frame stress by a factor of 16 with the .40 S&W.

The magazine release borrows from the P7 design with a latch on either side of the frame behind the trigger guard. This makes releasing a magazine a snap whether with the thumb or forefinger, a method that most lefties find just as, or even more, convenient than thumb release — and which right-handed users are more or less accustomed to (though the operation with this pistol is a bit different from the "button" release pioneered by John Moses Browning).

It should be noted that the release on the USP guns is a plastic molding. This works perfectly since it mates with the plastic magazines designed for the pistol. This wouldn't be the case with an aftermarket metal magazine modified to fit the gun; shooters (especially those with the limited-capacity "Clinton" magazine), must not be tempted to use a modified metal magazine designed for another gun with the USP. Doing so will eventually damage the magazine catch.

Magazines normally drop free when released. But should they remain in the pistol because of dirt, indentations on either side of the grip plate area permit grasping the edge of the magazine between thumb and forefinger. Numbered witness holes on the back of the magazine permit quick counting of the cartridges loaded in it.

Although the magazine is constructed mostly of plastic, the overall design is that of the classic magazine dating back to the early 1900s. For added strength a spring-steel metal insert reinforces the inside of the feed lips and inside top rear and sides of the magazine.

Due to the clause in the 1994 Crime Bill, manufacture of magazines with greater than 10-round capacity has virtually come to a halt; it seems likely that future magazines for the USP will continue to be offered with the limited capacity Clinton magazine.

These limited magazines have an extra-large spacer inside the bottom plate to restrict the capacity to 10 rounds. These should not be altered as long as the law is in effect. Obviously the full-capacity magazines are a better option if the shooter can locate them (and these can be purchased by law enforcement and government users of the pistol — with the law apparently designed to treat criminals and honest civilians in the same manner).

The USP 45 is nearly identical to the original USP guns in 9mm and .40. However the .45 ACP chambering dictates a larger frame and slide to accommodate the round. Operation and layout of controls on the pistol are identical to that of the .40 and 9mm guns.

Introduced in 1995, the USP 45 is being sold only with the 10-round magazine, even though it is designed to carry 12 rounds. As with its sister guns, this magazine should not be modified for greater than 10-round capacity unless the Federal law dictating reduced capacity is repealed. (Some law enforcement and government agencies are exempted from this ban.)

The .45 caliber version of the USP is not for everyone. Shooters with small hands will find that the trigger pull from the double-action mode is overly long and dictates a change from the normal hand position. However, if a single-action pull is used or shooters have medium to large hands, the pistol should fit well.

Heckler & Koch, Inc., has put its full efforts toward making all three versions of the USP suitable for a variety of users. And adding to this push is the addition of excellent accessories for the company's pistol. This task has been made simpler by

USP chambered for .45 Auto (bottom) shown with the model
1911A1 (top). (Photo courtesy of Heckler & Koch, Inc.)

the "accessory rail" that has thoughtfully been molded into the front of the frame.

Included in these accessories, is an excellent no-gunsmithing scope mount, a muzzle brake, laser sight, and flash light attachment. These make it possible to adapt the USP to a variety of shooting needs, whether contest or defensive. (A more detailed look at these accessories will be given in a subsequent chapter.)

Specifications for the USP (.40)

Caliber: .40 S&W
Overall length: 6.9 inches
Height: 5.25 inches
Width: 1.06 inches
Barrel length: 4.25 inches
Barrel rifling: Polygonal profile with right hand twist
Standard magazine capacity: 13 rounds
Weight empty: 28 ounces

Specifications for the USP (9mm)

Caliber: 9mm x 19 Parabellum (Luger)
Overall length: 6.9 inches
Height: 5.25 inches
Width: 1.06 inches
Barrel length: 4.25 inches
Barrel rifling: Polygonal profile with right hand twist
Standard magazine capacity: 15 rounds
Weight empty: 28 ounces

Specifications for the USP (.45)

Caliber: .45 ACP
Overall length: 7.87 inches
Sight Radius: 6.22 inches
Height: 5.55 inches
Width (slide): 1.14 inches
Wide (frame): 1.26 inches
Barrel length: 4.41 inches
Barrel rifling: Polygonal profile with right hand twist, 1 turn per 15.98 inches

Heckler & Koch's Handguns

Standard magazine capacity: 10 rounds (12 rounds, law
enforcement and military)
Weight, empty: 29.6 ounces
Magazine, empty: 1.17 ounces

USSOCOM

The USSOCOM pistol is part of a weapons system designed
for the U. S. military. The project was to create a special purpose pistol that could be employed with a silencer as well as
special infrared laser sighting system. The project was over-
seen by the U. S. Special Operations Command (USSOCOM)
which was working toward the adoption of a standard firearm
to be used by the Air Force Special Operations Wing, the U. S.
Rangers, the Navy SEALs, and the Green Berets, possibly with
input from other U. S. law enforcement and anti-terrorist units.

The pistols introduced for the testing had to meet the specifications set out by the U. S. military's Offensive Handgun
Weapons System project. Included in the specifications were
the .45 ACP chambering and an integral suppresser designed
for the pistol and a detachable laser sight.

Heckler & Koch entered its USSOCOM into the tests, working in conjunction with Insight Technology. The USSOCOM
pistol drew from the basic system Heckler & Koch had created
for the USP pistol which the company had on the drawing
boards. In effect, Heckler & Koch created the pistol and silencer systems while Insight Technology developed the LAM
(Laser Aiming Module), though both companies had to work
together in order to create a quick-on/quick-off design which
the military specified. By building on the foundation laid by
the USP development, the two companies were able to quickly
create an integrated, high-tech firearm/silencer/laser sight system that met or exceeded the government's specifications.

The silencer that Heckler & Koch created for the USSOCOM
was not as effective as military testers had hoped. Soon Knight's
Armament Company of Vero Beach, FL, was brought in to help
the Heckler & Koch team redesign its suppresser. The Knight's
Armament suppresser built on the tried-and-true tubular
suppresser design rather than the futuristic-looking, but less

Left-side view of USSOCOM pistol chambered for .45 Auto (Photo courtesy of Heckler & Koch, Inc.)

USSOCOM pistol with original modular laser aimer (below slide in front of trigger guard) and unorthodox rectangular suppresser. (Photo courtesy of Heckler & Koch, Inc.)

Heckler & Koch's Handguns

USSOCOM pistol shown with tear gas grenade and spare magazine. Insert shows the pistol with Laser Aiming Module and Knight's Armament Company suppresser which replaced the original created by Heckler & Koch. (Photo courtesy of Heckler & Koch, Inc.)

effective, rectangular silencer created by the Heckler & Koch engineers.

The USSOCOM has a high-strength polymer frame with steel mounting rails for added durability. The front of the frame is square with lines parallel to the sight radius of the pistol. This, coupled with mounting bars molded into the frame, makes it practical to mount a laser sight or other quick-detach assemblies.

The primary use of this mounting system is for attaching the "Laser Aiming Module" developed for the military's specifications. In addition to containing a laser sight, the module also acts as a flashlight, normally producing infrared light that can only be viewed with night vision goggles. This permits the user to employ the pistol/laser assembly both as a "flashlight" in total darkness as well as an aiming system when used in conjunction with night vision goggles.

Like the USP guns, most of the metal parts in the USSOCOM pistol are highly corrosion resistant. Coupled with the polymer frame, this makes the pistol highly resistant to rust, a big plus with a pistol that might be submerged in salt water during some SEAL military operations.

The USSOCOM pistol also utilizes the buffer system of the USP, reducing felt recoil in addition to extending the life of the

USSOCOM pistol. Insert shows the pistol with Knight's Armament Company suppresser. (Photo courtesy of Heckler & Koch, Inc.)

Heckler & Koch's Handguns

pistol itself. During USSOCOM military tests, individual Heckler & Koch pistols were fired in excess of 30,000 times using +P loads (producing more recoil and pressure than normal .45 ACP cartridges do) with no damage to any major components including the pistol's frame. Because the system is based simply on a heavier spring that reduces the slamming at the last part of the slide's recoil, it doesn't wear out or need maintenance.

Heckler & Koch, Inc. of Sterling , Virginia announced that on June 29, 1995 it was awarded a $4.5 million Phase III production contract from the U. S. Special Operations Command (USSOCOM), for an initial production order of 1,950 .45 caliber pistols and 10,140 magazines. The pistol has been officially classified as the MK23 MOD 0, USSOCOM Pistol, Semi-Automatic, Cal .45. The order was issued by the U. S. Navy Surface Warfare Center, Crane, Indiana for USSOCOM. The USSOCOM commands the elite Special Operations Forces which include the Navy SEALs, the Air Force Special Operations Wing, and the Army Special Forces, Rangers and Special Operations Aviation.

Under the terms of the Phase III order, the first production pistols and magazines were to be delivered to the Navy on May 1, 1996. Orders for additional pistols and spare magazines were expected by the end of 1995. Under the Phase III contract, a maximum of 7,500 pistols, 52,500 magazines and 1,950 suppressors may be procured, with a full potential contract value of $12 million.

Specifications for the USSOCOM

Caliber: .45 ACP
Overall length: 8.5 inches
Sight Radius: 6.8 inches
Height: 5.7 inches
Width (slide): 1.14 inches
Width (frame): 1.26 inches
Barrel length: 5 inches
Barrel rifling: Polygonal profile with right hand twist, 1 turn per 15.98 inches
Standard magazine capacity: 12 rounds
Weight, empty: 31 ounces
Magazine, empty: 1.17 ounces

HK PW (Personal Weapon)

The Heckler & Koch Personal Weapon is a proposed handgun chambering a shortened, caseless cartridge based on the larger caseless round created for Heckler & Koch's G11 rifle. The experimental pistol has a more or less conventional shape.

Because of the winding down of the Cold War and the reunification of Germany, it appears that work on the PW has been shelved until there might be a need for it. Consequently the PW appears to have never got beyond the conceptual stage.

With rifles and submachine guns getting smaller and special troops opting for more or less conventional pistol designs constructed with plastics and other materials (like the USSOCOM pistol), it seems likely that the PW or other similar pistols will not go into production in the foreseeable future. However, it is always hard to predict the future of firearms trends so the last may not have been seen of the PW concept.

Heckler & Koch's Handguns

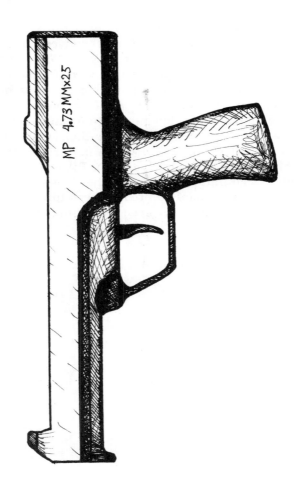

MP 4.73 MM×25

Proposed design for Heckler & Koch's "Personal Weapon" which would utilize a shorter, caseless cartridge similar to that of the G11 rifle.

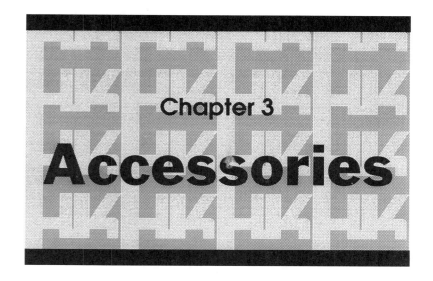

Chapter 3
Accessories

With the addition of tritium night sights or perhaps a scope mount and dot scope, the Heckler & Koch pistols are hard to improve. Many of the gadgets presently sold for various pistols don't do a lot to increase the reliability of a firearm and some gadgets lower the reliability of pistols—with disastrous results if the gun is for self-protection. Consequently the majority of shooters are better off purchasing ammunition and devoting their time in perfecting shooting skills rather than buying the latest gadgetry that may fail to deliver.

Quality ammunition is readily available from Olin/Winchester, Action Ammo, Federal Cartridge Company, Omark/CCI, Remington, Black Hills Ammunition, and PMC among others. These manufacturers and importers offer ammunition that's non-corrosive (unlike some of the surplus and Eastern-European ammunition that still occasionally shows up on the marketplace). And, when it comes to accuracy, these companies have excellent match grade ammunition that allows a shooter to take full advantage of the precision shooting offered by these pistols. For extended practice, PMC, Winchester, and Federal all offer low-cost "generic" ammunition.

During practice it's essential for shooters to employ ear and eye protection. In addition to preserving the gunner's senses, devices that protect the ears and eyes also help prevent the development of flinching when shots are fired — a habit that once established makes hitting the target almost impossible.

When laser sights, scopes, or other accessories are added to a pistol, care must be exercised because the end result may create more problems than are fixed. A laser sight, for example, may dictate a new holster to accommodate it. And that new holster might, in turn, dictate a new belt or make concealed carry impossible.

One addition or modification of a pistol can lead to a series of changes that can become expensive and may even lower the reliability of the firearm. This means that anyone adding accessories to a handgun or making modifications of any sort must carefully test each new configuration to make sure that nothing can go wrong at a critical moment. Failure to do such testing can spell disaster at a critical moment.

Carrying Cases

The hard plastic case that most Heckler & Koch pistols come in is ideal for storage and even transport of a handgun. The molded box fits the gun perfectly and the hard plastic exterior gives the firearm a maximum of protection. The box can be locked and has room for the spare magazine and cleaning kit that comes with the pistol. The only catch comes if the shooter has spare magazines, scopes the pistol, or makes other modifications; then the pistol won't fit its original container. In such a situation, an aftermarket carrying case may be ideal both for storing and transporting the pistol since it will protect the firearm from bumps and scratches as well as from rust and dirt. A case can also be employed for long-term storage of a firearm.

While most Heckler & Koch arms are quite rust resistant, it's wise to avoid using a plastic bag, vinyl pouch, or other sealed container for storage since these promote rust and tarnishing because air can't flow through the container. A burlap-weave pistol "rug" is a much better choice for storing a handgun since the fabric permits moisture to escape from around the gun, heading off a lot of potential problems with rust or tarnishing.

One excellent source for such cases is Michaels of Oregon whose Uncle Mike's "Sidekick Pistol Rugs" are sold in most gun stores. The thick Cordura nylon padded foam cases have a brushed lining that won't damage the finish on a pistol. These rugs come in assorted colors including black, tan, camouflage, and forest green with the small size rug being ideal for the P7 series and the medium size fitting most of the other models covered in this manual. (A small carbine size is dictated for the SP89 pistol.) Cost is $12 per rug with the small and medium sizes.

Compensators, Ports, and Muzzle Brakes

Compensators, ports, and muzzle brakes are most often seen on contest guns. A few are even appearing on "carry" guns these days and it seems likely that this trend will continue. Technically a compensator or gas port prevents the upward climb of the muzzle during recoil while a muzzle brake reduces felt recoil. But most of these devices actually counter both recoil and muzzle flip to varying extents. The benefits of these devices include both more comfort and quicker, accurate shooting since the sights can be brought back onto target more quickly after a shot is fired due to reduced barrel rise.

Compensators add length to a pistol and weight as well. This dictates the purchase of new holsters to accommodate the added length and any such pistol is going to be a bit more fatiguing to carry for long periods of time. The only exception to this rule is when ports are cut into the slide and barrel (as with Mag-na-porting). In such a case the pistol remains nearly the same as before.

Compensating guns is hardly a new concept. John Moses Browning was using diverted gas to power his early machine gun designs in the late 1800s and the first Thompson submachine guns of the 1920s sported Cutts compensators. But the current craze for compensated pistols can be traced to the 1970s when these devices started showing up on IPSCC guns where contestants employed compensators to help bring the muzzle of their pistols back onto target in a hurry, a prime requisite for winning contests.

Early compensators to appear in the 1970s were simply longitudinal ports cut into barrels extending an inch beyond the slide of the automatic. But soon the portion of the barrel extending beyond the slide was being encased in a muzzle weight for greater recoil reduction due to the inertia of the added weight; most of these compensators were simply a cylinder-shaped weight, often with ports, wrapped around the extended barrel. More aesthetically pleasing "full-profile" compensators appeared; these followed the contours of the slide, blending with its lines.

Other contest shooters tried adding weights to the front of the frame below the slide, often with a solid block of steel being welded to the front of the frame, creating a massive assembly toward the front of the gun. Like the weight of the compensators attached to barrels, this added weight fights against the recoil of the pistol.

Whether below the frame or on the barrel, as long as the added mass isn't on the slide, the "lock time" will not be affected. Lock time, the period of time before the barrel disengages from the slide, ejects an empty cartridge, and then rechambers a round and locks up the action, is an important consideration for contest shooters. If the lock time is slowed, critical second shots take longer to make. If the weight is added to the barrel or frame, the lock time doesn't become greater; if the weight is added to the slide, lock time increases. Consequently, the compensators contest shooters want is not something that attaches to the slide. Of course the downside to this is a much heavier gun—a pain if one has to carry the gun for long.

To get away from the added weight to a contest gun, compensators that divert gas to reduce recoil and barrel flip have become popular. Of these, the latest trick gunsmiths exploit is an "expansion chamber" next to the muzzle of the barrel followed by a narrowed exit hole for the bullet. Gas becomes compressed behind the bullet and exits the compensation slots with greater pressure, thereby increasing the downward deflection that operates against the muzzle rise. Gas pressure against the narrow exit hole of the compensator also reduces felt recoil in this design.

As noted above, compensated versions of the P7 and P9S pistols have been created with some being marketed by Heckler & Koch. The current thrust at Heckler & Koch seems to be toward marketing the USP as the "comp" gun in the company's lineup. The compensator is easily attached thanks to a modular "Quik-Comp" that attaches to the front of the USP, held in place on the universal mounting slot of the frame. Because many contest shooters also scope their pistols, the Quik-Comp is designed to permit mounting it in conjunction with the Heckler & Koch scope mount system.

The Quik-Comp is a muzzle brake/compensator that redirects gases through its expansion chamber that is just ahead of the muzzle of the barrel. The gas is then vented through ports to help reduce muzzle flip and reduce felt recoil by as much as 25 percent. In the process muzzle flash is also reduced.

USP in .40 S&W with Quik-Comp and Heckler & Koch's scope mount. (Photo courtesy of Heckler & Koch, Inc.)

Heckler & Koch's Handguns

The big plus of the Quik-Comp is that it doesn't require any modifications to the pistol; the barrel, frame, and slide all remain unchanged permitting a shooter to transform his standard "carry pistol" into a competition gun as the need presents itself. This system allows one gun to do the job of two. Cost of the Quik-Comp is $125.

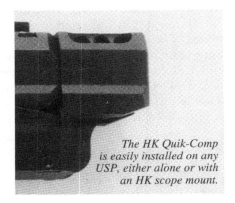

The HK Quik-Comp is easily installed on any USP, either alone or with an HK scope mount.

Close-up of Quik-Comp, showing ports that vent gas to reduce muzzle flip and recoil. (Photo courtesy of Heckler & Koch, Inc.)

Despite the fact that P7 and PSP pistols aren't currently readily available, the fixed barrels on these two firearms gives them a theoretical edge on potential accuracy. For this reason these handguns, especially the more readily available P7 series, are sometimes customized to create competition pistols. The best known of these guns are the handiwork of Les Pitman, working out of Custom Gun Services.

The Pitman compensator is created by welding a one-piece steel extension to the front of the slide. The barrel and gas system remain unaltered making this relatively efficient and less expensive than it might otherwise be.

Mag-na-port International employs a system that displaces metal electronically. This makes the "cuts" Mag-na-port makes to a pistol to create compensation ports very clean and smooth

Addition of Quik-Comp, scope mount, and scope transforms the USP into a competition pistol. (Photo courtesy of Heckler & Koch, Inc.)

without any damage to the pistol or changing in the tempering of the slide or barrel.

The big plus of the system is that recoil reduction and compensation takes place without any additional weight or length to the pistol. About the only downside is a very slight drop of muzzle velocity, though this is generally so slight as to be unnoticed in changes of point of impact or terminal ballistics. Cost varies according to the firearm, but is generally very competitive to custom work or the price of the Heckler & Koch Quik-Comp.

Flashlights and Flashlight Mounts

Just as lasers have "shrunk" thanks to technology, so have flashlights. Bulb brightness has increased while battery size became more compact. As the size has decreased and the brightness increased, some shooters have discovered that placing a very compact, high-intensity light on a pistol makes sense given the fact that the majority of shootouts occur in low-light environments.

A flashlight on a pistol helps the shooter determine who is friend or foe — something that can't easily be done with iron sights having tritium inserts or a laser sight. Since innocent bystanders or family members can be in areas that may be invaded by a criminal, a bright flashlight can not only identify a target, it can be a lifesaver by giving the user quick visual confirmation of friend or foe.

If a flashlight on a pistol is aligned with the point of aim, the flashlight can also serve as a crude aiming device, making it practical to ignore the sights when engaging a criminal at very close range. At longer ranges, the light will silhouette the iron sights, making possible targeting for very accurate shots in otherwise dark environments. Very bright flashlights even produce enough light to dazzle a criminal in the process of identifying him, giving the user a slight advantage over him.

The down side is that a flashlight shows exactly where the shooter is and makes a dandy target. Care has to be exercised with these devices, even when they're mounted on a firearm as a sighting system. As with the laser sight, it's important to only shine a flashlight for brief periods, then move to another location quickly in the darkness. To employ such tactics, a momentary switch that can be easily activated is a must for a flashlight mounted on any Heckler & Koch .

Flashlights also have a limited "range," quickly spreading out over any distance. Therefore flashlight "sights" are effective only with targets within 10 or 20 yards of the shooter with the advantage of the light quickly becoming a liability at greater ranges.

The added bulk of a flashlight on a pistol can also create problems, (though the mass can also act to reduce felt recoil, creating a compensator effect). And of course holster carry becomes almost impossible with some flashlight mounts (though newer, small flashlights can fit into holsters designed for laser-equipped pistols).

Currently the most ideal flashlight/pistol system in the Heckler & Koch lineup is the Universal Tactical Light (UTL) the company has created for its USP pistols. The UTL is compact and rugged and has a brilliant tungsten/halogen light superior to most handgun flashlights. The beam can also be adjusted to suit the shooter.

One big plus of the UTL is that it can be easily snapped on in a few seconds and locked on the universal mounting slot of the frame where a slide on the UTL will keep it put. And the UTL can be quickly removed by sliding the lock down and snapping the light off. (About the only downside of the UTL is that it can't be used with the scope mount or muzzle brake systems which mount to the universal slot of the USP.)

The light has a master power switch that can be set to an on or off position. In the "on" position, the shooter can toggle the switch (with either his trigger finger or the index finger of his off hand) to turn the light on momentarily (by sliding the switch to the right) or to lock the light on (by toggling it to the left). This switch design coupled with the ability to quickly attach and detach the light makes for a very flexible system. For added flexibility, Heckler & Koch offers an optional momentary switch

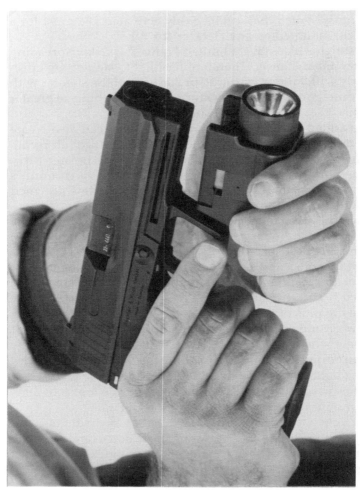

The UTL can be quickly mounted or removed on the USP with a simple rocking twist and activation of the slide locker. (Photo courtesy of Heckler & Koch, Inc.)

The compact UTL adds little in length and weight to the HK USP.

Side view of UTL mounted on USP. (Photo courtesy of Heckler & Koch, Inc.)

that can be plugged into the UTL and positioned on the pistol's grip.

The light can be focused and uses two lithium Duracell 123A batteries which give up to 30 minutes of continuous running time. The UTL weighs only 5.3 ounces so the weight is hardly noticeable on the already lightweight USP. Cost of the UTL is $225.

A shooter should be able to employ the light almost instinctively to illuminate his target, fire if necessary, and then avoid possible return fire by switching the light off and quickly moving to another position. Otherwise the shooter may experience a "terminal" failure of his tactics when using the UTL or other flashlight in a gunfight.

Heckler & Koch also offers a belt pouch for carrying the UTL. This pouch also permits pointing the light forward while still on the belt to illuminate an area with the need to point the pistol toward the target while keeping both hands free. The pouch can also be used to mount the UTL on shotguns or rifles.

UTL with light "locked on." (Photo courtesy of Heckler & Koch, Inc.)

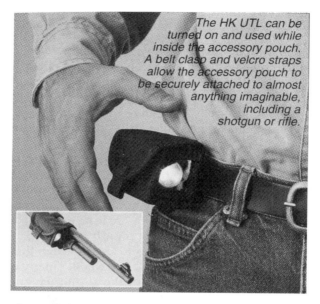

The HK UTL can be turned on and used while inside the accessory pouch. A belt clasp and velcro straps allow the accessory pouch to be securely attached to almost anything imaginable, including a shotgun or rifle.

UTL can be switched on in its belt carrying pouch. Insert shows how the pouch design permits attaching the light to shotguns or other long arms as well. (Photo courtesy of Heckler & Koch, Inc.)

Grip Panels

Many popular pistols with removable grip plates have replacement grips of exotic woods or walnut available for them as well as a variety of synthetic grip plates ranging from synthetic ivory to rubberized plastic. Unfortunately the Heckler & Koch pistols, perhaps because they are mostly purchased by users who are professionals for the most part, haven't produced enough demand for replacement grips to entice any of the major manufacturers to tool up for such accessories.

Such grips can be made on a custom basis, but such expense is either out of the reach of most shooters or the owners of the gun already have an it's-fine-as-is attitude about the grips on their handguns. And the molded grip panels that are integral on the frame of the USP also dictate against any possibility of replacement panels for this gun.

Heckler & Koch's Handguns

There is one inexpensive alternative to altering the grip of the Heckler & Koch pistols. This is the rubberized sleeve several manufacturers have created. These sleeves slip around the grip, changing its contour and also giving a much different surface for the shooter to hang onto. Since some shooters feel that the rubber adds a little recoil reduction and some like the added traction the rubber gives, this is an option some may wish to consider.

On the downside, a slip-on grip adds girth to a pistol since the sleeve goes over the grip rather than replacing it; this is far from ideal for those with small hands. But many shooters with larger hands may choose a sleeve because of its finger grooves around the front of the pistol frame, creating a very secure hold that brings the gun back on target rapidly.

Hogue offers the "Handall" soft rubber sleeve that will fit the USP pistols. These sleeves will also fit over many of Heckler & Koch's other pistols. Cost of the slip-on Hogue grip is $10. Michaels of Oregon offers a black slip-on grip sleeve that has checkering on its side and two finger swells on its front strap. The company's full-size version of this grip (product number 59603) fits most of the Heckler & Koch pistols. Cost is $19 per sleeve.

Handi-Hider

The "Handi-Hider" from Choate Machine & Tool is a small metal bar welded to a plate with four screw holes in it. This plate can be attached to walls, under a table, or a variety of other places permitting sliding a pistol onto it, with the vinyl-coated rod slipping into the barrel. This enables a gun owner to hide a Heckler & Koch pistol in a variety of out-of-sight places while still having the pistol close by, ready to be grabbed and brought into play in an instant.

Obviously care must be exercised to avoid hiding the gun where a child might discover it; but this system is ideal for many businessmen who want to have a gun handy in case of a hold up while not frightening gun-shy customers. And homeowners often discover that the Handi-Hider is perfect for keeping a gun close to the bed, ready to deal with a burglar. The Handi-

Holder costs $7.50 with models available with 90 or 45 degree post angles and rod diameters of 9mm, 40 S&W, or .45 available.

Holsters

Untold pistols are carried worldwide in the so-called "Mexican Holster" (i.e., carrying a pistol inside the waistband of the shooter's pants). As one might imagine, this is convenient only in terms of the initial cost of the holster. Many accidents occur with this style of carry and not a few guns are lost — or snatched out of the waistband by an opponent. Worse yet, guns sometimes slip down a trouser leg for a totally embarrassing situation.

Although excellent leather holsters are available for all of the Heckler & Koch guns (with the exception of the SP89 which is better suited to a shoulder strap for carrying), leather holsters are generally expensive and don't protect a firearm as well as nylon and Cordura holsters do. Consequently a shooter is advised to first try out a holster made of these synthetic materials since they're tough and don't promote corrosion — and are inexpensive to boot.

For those dissatisfied with synthetic holsters for one reason or another, some quality leather holsters are available. DeSantis, Milt Sparks, Alessi, and Triple K all offer excellent leather rigs that are hard to beat and which are molded to fit guns exactly.

As for synthetic holsters, there is a wide variety to choose from. Brigade Quartermaster markets a number of nylon holsters and accessories designed for military, police, and civilian users. The company's "Quickfire" consists of a nylon holster that can be adjusted for large and small pistols thanks to a Velcro strap and an open base. The Quickfire uses a thumb break strap so a pistol carried in it is very secure; cost is $15.

Police or other shooters interested in the low-slung SAS-type holster will find Brigade Quartermasters' "Hi-Tac Assault Holster" to their liking. The flapped holster comes with all the straps needed to sling it from a belt and a secondary strap to secure it to the shooter's thigh. Fastex buckles and Velcro allow easy mounting and adjustment of the holster and a magazine pouch along its front edge makes it easy to carry spare ammunition. The black nylon pouch is padded and waterproofed; the price is $50.

Brigade Quartermasters' "Archangel" is similar to the Hi-Tac but lacks the front magazine pouch and flap and costs $40. For those selecting the SAS MK IV or the Hi-Tac, the company also offers the "SAS Flash-Bang Belt/Leg Pouch" which can be worn on the off-hand side, hanging from the belt and strapped to the leg to accommodate three fragmentation or smoke grenades; cost is $45.

Possibly the best bargain in the synthetic holster market is from Michaels of Oregon. The "Uncle Mike's" police and civilian holsters are constructed of tough Cordura; they're also readily available at many gun stores making them easy to purchase. Uncle Mike's belt holsters fit most belts or can be worn on the company's inexpensive "Sidekick Holster Belts" designed for them. These belts have a quick release buckle making it easy to adjust and put on; they're available in brown, black, and camo. Cost is $8 apiece.

Uncle Mike's "Sidekick" holster has an adjustable snap strap to secure the gun. Sandwiched between the inner and outer skin of the holster is a thick, waterproof foam padding that makes the holster conform to the gun carried in it for a "custom fit." Available in black or camo finishes, the price for the Sidekick holster is $15.

For police and security guards, Uncle Mike's "Duty Holster" with thumb-break snap is ideal; cost is $30. Uncle Mike's "Duty System" series of pouches and accessories is also offered for policemen; various pouches in this series are designed to hold magazines, radios, mace, batons, flashlights, handcuffs, and keys. For the ultimate in police carry, Uncle Mike's has created the "Pro-3" line of Duty holsters; this is reinforced with plastic and has a tough thumb break retainer strap.

Uncle Mike's reversible (left or right hand) horizontal shoulder harness holster is ideal for concealed carry under a jacket. The "Horizontal Shoulder" with two straps crossing in the back, or the "Undercover Horizontal" using the more conventional method of looping the off-hand strap over the shoulder and back across the lower back (for superior concealment) are both ideal. Cost for the Horizontal Shoulder holster is $30 while the Undercover Horizontal retails at $25.

Concealing a pistol on a belt is considerably more comfortable than shoulder harness systems. Uncle Mike's black "Super Belt Slide" pancake holster is ideal for such carry and is offered for $18. The company also sells an ultra-thin "Inside-the-Pant" holster which clips to the belt; this holster is available in both a thumb-break and non-thumb-break style. Uncle Mike's "Ankle Holster", selling for $27, will accommodate the smaller Heckler & Koch pistols but should never be used with full-size guns.

In addition to holsters, Uncle Mike's single and double magazine pouches, fanny packs, and other pouches designed for hunting and outdoor use, are all designed to match the finish of the company's Sidekick holsters and belts.

Those who add a larger laser sight under the barrel of their Heckler & Koch pistol need a special holster designed to accommodate the larger bulk of the entire assembly. Fortunately two such holsters are available. Adventurer's Outpost sells a "Universal Pistol Laser Holster" for laser-sighted Heckler & Koch pistols. Constructed of black ballistic nylon, the "PLH-R" is the right-hand model and the "PLH-L" is the left-hand model. Both have thumb-break straps and cost $30 each.

Uncle Mike's product line includes a holster designed to accommodate an under-the-barrel laser. This holster is available in black, and it has a thumb-break safety similar to that of the company's duty holster. Cost is $30.

For those needing a competition holster, things have been bleak in the past with most manufacturers aiming for majority of contestants shooting 1911-style comp guns. But this has changed with the introduction of Bianchi International's "Gilmore Speed Leader" holster which was designed by competition champ Riley Gilmore. This holster is adjustable in ten different areas, accommodating a variety of barrel lengths and styles of guns. And Milt Sparks and Alessi also fabricate comp holsters designed for contest shooting, tailoring the holster to the shooter's firearm.

Safariland has also created several "Paddle Holsters" which will accommodate scoped pistols. These holsters are made of a laminate plastic which locks itself around the pistol. The holster itself is designed to be worn with its inner section inside the waistband, doing away with the need for a belt to hold it in place. A Belt Loop Accessory can be purchased for it for $8.50 for those wishing a more traditional carry. These Safariland holsters are available from Ed Brown Products and the cost is $47 per holster.

"Butt pack" style holsters are also available. Given the popularity of these pouches with joggers and tourists, this makes an ideal holster for those wanting to carry a pistol without alarming those around them. Care has to be exercised with these holsters, however, because pistols carried in them are considered "concealed" in many areas of the U.S. Probably the best and least expensive of these is Uncle Mike's "GunRunner Fanny Pack" style holster can conceal even a full-sized Heckler & Koch pistol (though the P7 series is better suited to such carry). For undercover detectives, the pouches even come with a badge holder.

Regardless of what style of holster is adopted, a shooter should spend a lot of time becoming familiar with it, practicing until snaps or other fasteners can be operated smoothly and the firearm presented quickly (with the finger not going into the trigger guard until the gun is on target). A shooter is also wise to always wear pistol holsters so they place the gun in the same location on the belt or under the shoulder. Switching carry positions from shoulder carry to side carry, for example, can cause a shooter to draw for his pistol in an emergency, only to discover that it's on his belt. Habits are hard to break; and habits take over during an emergency — especially when a person is trying to defend himself.

"Butt pack" style holster in the Uncle Mike's lineup offers in-
the-open concealability.   (Photo courtesy of Michaels of
Oregon Company.)

Iron Sights

Pistol scopes (see below) can get complicated and expensive. They add weight to a pistol and make it a chore to carry. Consequently shooters with good eyesight who have to carry a pistol for any length of time generally opt for iron sights. Unlike laser, dot, or optical sights, iron sights don't add a lot of bulk to a handgun.

Since the majority of gunfights occur at night or in poorly lit areas, nightsights (iron sights with glow-in-the-dark inserts) make a lot of sense. These sights assist in locating a target in dim light.

Most modern night sights contain small glass vials of tritium gas (an isotope of hydrogen); these tiny containers are inserted into small holes drilled in the front and on either side of the rear sight notch. Tritium sights give bright glowing points of light that are easily aligned with a target in the darkest of environments. The life of the radioactive material is such that the dots will remain bright and useable at night for at least 10 years before need for replacement.

Radioactive things make most thinking people a bit squirmy. But tritium is very safe since no radiation other than visible light penetrates the glass vial containing the radioactive gas. And even if a vial of a tritium sight breaks indoors—an occurrence that is hard to imagine unless the sight were abused—the exposure to radiation is minimal since the gas quickly dissipates into the atmosphere — though to be on the safe side, the room should be aired out if such an accident occurs.

Heckler & Koch offers tritium night sights for its USP and P7 series of guns. These sights are available with a choice of orange, yellow or green rear sight inserts (that are to either side of the blade cutout) coupled with a green front sight. Cost is $88 per set. Sights are available for all the USP pistols and all except the older P7PSP in the P7 series of guns.

In addition to night sights offered by Heckler & Koch for its two top-of-the-line pistols, there are a variety of aftermarket iron sights and night sights available for many of the company's pistols. Probably the best source for these is Brownells which carries many of the sights listed below.

Heckler & Koch's tritium night sights. (Photo courtesy of Heckler & Koch, Inc.)

Meprolight night sights designed for MP5 will also fit SP89 pistol. (Photo courtesy of Hesco, Inc.)

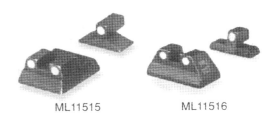

Meprolight night sights designed for USP and P7 pistols. (Photo courtesy of Hesco, Inc.)

Heckler & Koch's Handguns

Millett offers an adjustable rear sight for the P7 pistols which must be used in conjunction to Millett's front sight. The rear sight adjusts both for elevation and windage with miniature screws located on the sight. The Millett rear sight blade has a white outline (which shooters can blacken if they dislike it). Cost for the rear sight is $34.60. The required front sight is available in a choice of white or orange for $16 each; like the rear sight, the front can be darkened with a dab of paint if the shooter dislikes having a colored insert on his sight.

Israeli Military Industries has developed a series of tritium sights for a variety of firearms. The U. S. distributor, Hesco, Incorporated, markets these as the "Meprolight" sights and the company carries sights for the MP5 submachine guns; these sights also fit the SP89. Purchasers can choose between buying a tritium-insert front sight (product number ML31505) for $50 or a front and rear sight with inserts (ML31506) in both for $95. Hesco also offers fixed front/rear sight kits for the USP (ML11516) as well as the P7M8, and P7M13 (ML11515) for $95 per set.

Whether night sights or standard iron sights are used on a pistol, they aren't of much use if not properly zeroed. Fortunately the sights on Heckler & Koch pistols will have been zeroed at the factory and shouldn't be adjusted unless, for some reason, they are not on the mark — a situation that may occur with a change of ammunition or when the shooter has a hold that differs somewhat from the norm.

Fortunately even fixed sights are easily adjusted for windage and — with a bit of labor — for elevation. Before zeroing, it's wise to choose the type of ammunition that will most often be fired from the gun and zero the sights with that ammunition to avoid the changes that can occur when switching from one type of ammunition to another.

A pistol that shoots low and which has non-adjustable sights can be altered to zero it. This entails "lowering" the front sight by removing metal from its top to raise the group. If the pistol shoots high, filing the rear sight's notch and top edge will lower the group. Obviously this work needs to be done cautiously since once the metal is removed, it's impossible to put it back. It's wise to have a gunsmith handle the task, though most do-it-yourselfers can tackle the job with some success if they do the work in stages, carefully test firing the pistol as the work progresses.

Guns having sights that can be adjusted for elevation make zeroing an easier task. The rule is to raise the rear sight to raise the group and lower the sight to lower the group. To help out, most adjustable sights will be marked with an "E" for elevation and an arrow showing the "UP" direction needed to raise groups.

Bullet impact can be "moved" to one side slightly by drifting the rear sight. Drift adjustments are a possibility for do-it-yourselfers employing a drift punch or wooden peg placed against the sight and lightly tapped with a hammer. To adjust the windage of a fixed rear sight, move it opposite to the direction of the change in impact desired. If, for example, the Heckler & Koch pistol shoots to the right of the point of aim, the rear sight should be drifted to the left. With adjustable sights, moving the sight to the left moves the point of aim to the right (shifting groups to the left); moving the rear sight to the left moves the groups to the right. Usually the sight will be marked with an "L" or "R" to show which way to turn the micrometer screw to shift the group impact area.

Laser Sights

Once only a Buck Roger comic strip device, lasers in sights or elsewhere are today somewhat "ho-hum" to many shooters. For the uninitiated, a laser produces a tight beam of coherent light that travels in a straight line; a bullet's path is a shallow arch due to gravity and air resistance. While two such different paths only have points that match up once or twice at the most, the paths are within inches of each other within several hundred yards. And that type of accuracy is better than most shooters can realize, especially at longer ranges making the laser as a sighting device.

Modern laser sights have elevation and windage screws much like those of optical scopes; this makes it simple to zero them to a pistol's bore. The shooter employs the pistol's iron sights to aim at the target, turns on the laser, and notes where its beam strikes on the target, adjusting the laser accordingly until its beam hits at the same point as the iron sights target.

Lasers do have some disadvantages, especially in combat since the laser can be readily seen by an opponent. And in the daylight, most lasers aren't bright enough to be seen unless used with special targets—though this may be changing as we'll see in a moment. This means that lasers are only practical for self defense in very limited conditions: At night, indoors, or during dusk.

Group use of laser sights isn't practical at this point, either. If each person in a squad has a laser sight, it becomes almost impossible in combat to tell which aiming point belongs to whom. (Eventually "coded" pulsed lasers that have a computer control coupled to a blocking visor might be possible. Carefully timed to other users' lasers and visors, these might make it possible for each user to see only his laser dot. But such technology would be costly and the added bulk would seemingly make such gear less than ideal, at least with today's technology.)

Obviously great care has to be exercised so laser sights are employed to best tactical advantage. But within ideal operating environments, a laser sight on one of the Heckler & Koch pistols can be very effective and fast in bringing the firearm onto target. Too, a shooter doesn't need to bring his pistol to eye level and can fire with both eyes wide open without fear of an inaccurate shot with a laser sight. All he has to do is place the laser dot on the target, keep the firearm steady, and fire.

Because heroes in action movies often have laser sights— and almost never miss the target —the intimidation factor of a laser sight is currently great among criminals who face a laser sight. This intimidation factor creates an added tactical advantage.

Of course a laser sight isn't going to make everyone cower in terror. And as more combatants get used to seeing these sights in action, and realize that they aren't necessarily more accurate than standard sights, especially if the shooter hasn't practiced much with them, then the intimidation factor is going to drop off. But in the meantime, it's something to keep in mind and exploit if you have a laser mounted on a defensive weapon.

Because of the potential for eye damage, commercial laser sights are limited in power by the U. S. Federal Government; 5 milliwatts is the federal maximum. But that's all the power needed since a 5-milliwatt laser produces a dot that can be readily seen in dim light for several hundred yards—farther than the useful range of pistols. Range isn't the only factor to consider, however. While less powerful laser sights work well, many pistol shooters have opted to use full-power 5-milliwatt laser sights because the brighter beam is more easily seen in areas bordering on daylight. The larger 5 milliwatt laser sight makes the laser sight practical in brighter environments.

Most lasers aren't readily visible in daylight, in part because of their low power but also because the red wavelength is hard to see in the sunlight. As lasers become available in other wavelengths, this may change. Several manufacturers have recently introduced a "day" laser sights that shorten the wavelength down from the standard 670 nm (nanometer) wavelength of most lasers to 635 nm. While the result of a shorter wave isn't exactly brilliant in sunlight, it is visible under conditions when the standard 670 nm lasers are invisible and when shined on a reflective surface, can be seen even in sunlight. This makes it possible to sight the pistol in during the day if special reflective targets are exploited (these targets are available from most manufacturers offering 635nm lasers).

If the trend toward shorter wavelength lasers were to continue, the limitation of these sights to very dark environments might be less of a consideration, though it's doubtful that any laser with only 5mw of power will be visible in bright sunlight at any great range.

Military and police users sometimes find infrared laser sights useful. These have the added advantage of being visible only with night vision goggles, making them invisible to most opponents while being easily visible to those with the specialized equipment. In such a situation the laser sights can be employed without detection—provided an opponent isn't also wearing night vision goggles. (For a more detailed look at laser aiming devices as well as night vision gear, see *Lasers Sights and Night Vision Devices*, available from Desert Publications for $29.95.

Battery life varies according to the power of the laser sight and size of the battery supply, but most 3 milliwatt laser batteries will last up to 50 hours during continuous use before they need new batteries. Full-power lasers generally wear out batteries considerably sooner.

A laser sight beam is readily noticeable when it's in operation; good tactics dictate only switching it on long enough to acquire the target and fire. To do this, a momentary switch is used with most laser sights with the switch mounted on the grip of the pistol. Most laser sights have momentary switches for this purpose, though a few have only an on/off switch.

These latter sights do away with the awkward wire connecting momentary switches to their lasers, but shooters must learn to aim their pistol straight down or into the air after firing to avoid having the beam give away their position to their target when he returns fire. (It should also be noted that laser beams are especially noticeable in smoke, fog, or rain so great care must be exercised with these sights in combat environments like these.)

The momentary switch on lasers creates a few problems when mounting the system on a pistol. If care isn't taken, the wire connecting the switch to the laser can stick out, potentially ready to snarled in brush, or extend into the slide area of the pistol, creating the possibility of a jam at a critical moment.

Shooters sometimes opt for a standard off/on switch on the laser, even though it has the tactical disadvantages mentioned above, to get away from the wire-connected momentary switch. Others try to tape the switch to the grip of the gun, discovering the hard way that most tape oozes its adhesive over time or dissolves in cleaning solvents, creating a sticky mess on the firearm. One viable solution to the problem is to use black wire wraps (similar to those used on bread wrappers) to tie the cable to the underside of the trigger guard and then mount the momentary switch to the grip with Superglue.

More permanent laser mounts can be created with epoxy putty—at the risk of damaging the gun when the assembly has to be removed for one reason or another. A few shooters have even experimented with large black rubber "O" ring washers and rubber bands with varying results. With experimentation most shooters eventually come up with a solution, though it seems there is no really good system of mounting the momentary switch on the pistol grip at a convenient location without having wires or fasteners protrude from the firearm.

Heckler & Koch has done away with the wire/epoxy/tape madness with the introduction of 'wireless" switches which employ a low-power transmitter in a switch that can be mounted on the firearm. This transmitter has a range of only two feet; that's more than enough to reach the laser receiver mounted on a pistol. The system has been patented by Applied Laser Systems which supplies the lasers and their transmitter switches for the USP and SP89 pistols. The wireless laser for the USP clamps onto the pistols universal mounting slot. The SP89 laser mounts in the front sight base assembly of the pistol.

Wireless laser sight designed for USP. (Photo courtesy of Heckler & Koch, Inc.)

Heckler & Koch's Handguns

Wireless laser sight designed for SP89. (Photo courtesy of Heckler & Koch, Inc.)

Perhaps the handiest removable laser sight to date for pistols is the B-Square "Mini-Laser" which boasts a full 5 milliwatts of power in a compact size, only 1.1-inch square by a half inch, and a light weight of only a tad over 1 ounce with its batteries and remote switch. This laser attaches to many of the Heckler & Koch pistols with a universal mount that fits around the trigger guard.

The Mini-Laser is available in blued or stainless finish models with a choice of either an on/off switch that mounts on the laser just ahead of the trigger guard or a momentary switch on a cord. In addition to its compact size, the Mini-Laser has several added pluses. One is that it can be easily removed from its mount thanks to locking detents; it's also possible to replace the batteries in the sight without removing it from the gun. These two design features make for a very flexible system that's easy to keep zeroed to the gun. Cost is $300 for a blued Mini-Laser with cord or switch and $309 for the stainless model.

Tac-Star Industries has recently introduced its "Universal" series of lasers which are designed to fit virtually all handguns,

BSL Laser Sight Options

31000	**BSL: Cord Switch,** Blue	
31001	**BSL: Cord Switch,** Stainless	
31002	**BSL: Integral Switch,** Blue	
31003	**BSL: Integral Switch,** Stainless	

B-Square's BSL Laser sight and momentary switch, shown here with mounting brackets, wrenches for mounting and zeroing the laser. Tube in background is the shipping case. (Photo courtesy of Heckler & Koch, Inc.)

including most of the Heckler & Koch pistols (with the exception of the SP89). The standard Universal laser sight costs $119 and has a 5mw output. The Universal "2000" model costs $199 and has a 635 nm wavelength making it useful in brighter light.

Both of the Universal laser sights can be operated by a remote pressure switch for easy off/on use. The laser sights weigh 12 ounces with batteries, use three A76 batteries and operate for 45 minutes of continuous use before depleting the batteries. The laser sights are 2.43 inches long with a 0.55-inch diameter.

The Universal laser sights mount on the front of a pistol's trigger guard. Two bolts permit clamping the sight in place and, if aligned carefully, the sight can then be zeroed in the conventional manner.

Heckler & Koch's Pulse Beam laser sight was designed for its MP5 series of machine guns. This sight will also work on the SP89 if a portion of the handguard is removed to accommodate the laser. Due to the growing collector's value of the SP89, such alterations are probably best avoided; this makes the wireless laser offered by Heckler & Koch a better choice since it doesn't require alteration of the pistol's handguard.

Heckler & Koch's Handguns

PULSE BEAM Model 100 Laser Sight mounted on an HK SP 89 pistol with modified foream

Heckler & Koch's MP5 Pulse Beam laser sight. (Photo courtesy of Heckler & Koch, Inc.)

Regardless of the brand of laser mounted on a pistol, it is not a magical device that makes every bullet reach the exact spot the shooter was aiming for. To achieve accuracy with a laser sight, a shooter must practice and learn to hold his firearm steady and on target during the full pull of the trigger.

Magazines

Magazines are the most significant part of a semiauto pistol in terms of reliability since damaged magazines are the source of most pistol malfunctions. Magazines must be properly protected and shooters should take pains to never do anything which might scratch or alter the feed lips of a magazine.

A magazine that is incorrectly dimensioned or poorly made will also create a variety of failures. Because of the close tolerances between the Heckler & Koch pistol and its magazines, shooters needing new magazines should first consider purchasing them directly from Heckler & Koch whenever possible.

The Clinton Administration's 1994 Crime Bill has led to the 10-round maximum magazine that has come to be known as the "Clinton magazine". From the time the bill was finally signed into law, the manufacture of magazines with capacities over 10 rounds was made illegal, thereby assuring that only criminals and law enforcement officials would have access to new magazines after this cutoff date. About the only result of the law to date has been that it is harder and more expensive for honest folks to get pre-ban replacement magazines for their high-capacity pistols.

Fortunately, after telling Congress that it was essential to get the bill into law as soon as possible to stop mounting crime rates (actually the crime rates were dropping during this period), Clinton went on vacation without signing the bill into law for three weeks. During that time huge numbers of magazines were made by enterprising manufacturers who are now making a killing selling these magazines at exorbitant prices.

While the law limiting the capacity of newly made magazines may be repealed in the near future, shooters are well advised to purchase magazines as soon as they can because it is possible they may become scarce in the future. The only exception to the ban is with magazines made for the military or the police, suggesting that a brisk black market will develop in these magazines if other contraband black market sales of the past is any indication.

More good news is the fact that magazines that are properly cared for last almost forever. If stored loaded for long periods of time, quality magazine springs won't get a set that keeps them from feeding ammunition reliably. Such a happenstance is rare and generally occurs only with cheap magazines or those created when a country is at war and the spring hasn't been properly heat treated. (On the other hand, the polymer of the magazines does expand slightly when a magazine is loaded and may be the exception to this rule — only time will tell with this.)

Many a competition shooter drops an empty magazine out of his pistol to make way for rapidly inserting a full one. While this is great for speed, it can damage the magazines that are dropped. One way to protect them is to add a bumper pad to the base of the magazine.

Pachmayr magazine pads are currently offered by Brownells in sets of 5 with the "MBK-59" ideal for Heckler & Koch double-column magazines; cost is $15 per set of five. Contact cement is the easiest and best way to attach bumper pads to the floor plate of a magazine.

Magazine Pouches

Since the magazine is critical to the proper functioning of any pistol and high-capacity magazines are becoming more and more scarce, it's important to carry magazines in a pouch or other container that protects them. A bump or drop on the lip of a magazine can quickly turn it into a piece of junk; some lint picked up in a pocket can cause a jam when it and a cartridge try to share space in the chamber of a barrel. The best protection for a spare magazine is to carry it in a quality magazine pouch.

Good bets for magazine pouches are either military surplus or Uncle Mike's double magazine pouches, both of which are ideal for carrying most Heckler & Koch magazines. The Uncle Mike's pouches are available in both camouflage and black and fit perfectly on the company's belts; price is $14 per pouch.

Contest shooters, especially those using Safariland paddle holsters, will want to consider the Safariland "Paddle Magazine Holder" since it matches the holster and also doesn't require a belt to hold it in place, making it very quick to put on or take off. Each holder is constructed from a molded polymer that holds a magazine securely while still allowing it to be pulled from the top of the holder without unfastening any flaps, snaps, or Velcro tabs. This makes it ideal for competition, though not so suitable for self-defense purposes.

Scopes and Mounts

Most Heckler & Koch pistols have a greater potential accuracy right out of the box than their owners can take advantage of. Consequently, mounting an optical sight or other quality sighting system on one of these guns makes sense, especially with a pistol that will be used for hunting or contest shooting. For those with some types of vision problems, a pistol-mounted scope can also give a clearer view of the target and sights.

Whether a shooter adds a laser sight, optical scope, or even a flashlight to his pistol, there are some tradeoffs, because most of these make a handgun an awkward piece of equipment to carry. A pistol that was light and handy becomes a heavy, clumsy piece of machinery when an optical sight, large laser site, or other appendage is bolted to it. (This situation is gradually changing as more plastics and miniaturization come into play with these accessories. Consequently the additional weight and size of optical additions to pistols may be less of a concern in the near future.)

Such additions also dictate either a custom or competition holster, with the latter creating a whole new range of problems since scopes are relatively fragile and are exposed to the environment with most such holsters. A scope's extra bulk also ordains that there's more weight to carry and lift to bring the gun onto target, not minor considerations for those carrying the pistol around all day or doing a lot of shooting at the range.

Iron sights are often the best, cheapest, and most compact solution to bringing a gun onto target for most shooters. Telescopic sighting systems can be fast if a shooter puts in practice with them; but slight movements of a shooter's hand and the relatively narrow fields of view presented by most scopes makes quickly finding a target less than ideal. Scopes, like iron sights, require a lot of practice before a shooter really becomes proficient with them.

For shooters who have shot and practiced with iron sights for many years, another problem occurs when scoping a pistol; the gun is habitually raised to bring the iron sights to eye level. When a scope is on the pistol, this habit dictates a second motion to adjust the gun lower, aligning the scope to the eye — taking up a precious fraction of a second in the process. Because of this latter complication, many seasoned shooters find it takes a lot of extra practice before they can overcome old habits to bring a pistol on target with a scope as fast as they can with iron sights. These factors can cause critical extra moments

Heckler & Koch's Handguns

before the crosshairs get on target if a shooter is unfamiliar with the scope system. Obviously defensive use of a scoped pistol dictates aiming that has become a reflex. Anything less can get a gunner killed by his opponent.

A poor shooter with standard pistol will still be a poor shooter with a scoped pistol. But if enough practice is put into aiming a scoped Heckler & Koch pistol, it can pay off in increased shooting skills for many shooters.

On the other hand, scopes may be the best option for shooters with some types of eye problems or who regularly compete in shooting contests where scopes and lots of practice start to pay off in speed.

For hunters there is an added plus with optical scopes. The magnification makes identifying the target easier and bullet placement more precise.

There are several good scope-mount systems available for mounting scopes to many of the Heckler & Koch pistols. And many gunsmiths can quickly fabricate a pistol mount system for models of Heckler & Koch guns without a stock mount available. Once in place, the mounts provide a rock solid fastening point for the standard Weaver rings that will accommodate most pistol scopes.

In order to create a "contest" pistol for its product line, Heckler & Koch has taken advantage of the universal mounting slot on its USP pistols with several accessories that can be quickly fastened to the slot. Among these is a scope mount assembly, a "Quik-Comp" compensator, and a Universal Tactical Light flashlight assembly (these latter two devices are covered elsewhere in this publication).

The USP scope mount can be installed alone or with the company's Quik-Comp assembly, making it possible to quickly transform a standard USP into a pistol suitable for contest shooting. With the .40 S&W or .45 ACP chambering, this has the added benefit of putting the USP in the "major" category in many contests, giving the shooter an edge in scoring points.

The Heckler & Koch mount requires no modification to the pistol and simply bolts onto the grooved frame, an operation the owner can easily carry out. The mount accepts standard

Heckler & Koch's scope mount is ideal for the USP pistol. This pistol also sports the company's Quik-Comp compensator. Scope is an Aimpoint 3000 dot scope. (Photo courtesy of Heckler & Koch, Inc.)

Weaver rings so a variety of optical and dot pistol scopes as well as lasers and similar devices can be used with the USP. Additionally the mount is raised slightly so the iron sights can still be used if needed. This latter feature also makes disassembly of the pistol without removing the scope mount a practical operation. Cost of the Heckler & Koch scope mount is $170.

B-Square offers a "blued" model (actually black-finished aluminum) for the USP series of guns. This unit clamps to the universal mounting grooves of the frame and has enough clearance between the scope base mount and the slide to permit disassembly of the pistol without removing the sight — a big plus for many shooters.

Heckler & Koch's Handguns

The B-Square mount sits forward on the pistol (especially when compared to the Heckler & Koch scope mount attachment) making the chances of a stovepipe jam a very remote possibility, even if the pistol failed to eject a cartridge to the side — itself a very improbable occurrence. The B-Square mount sells for $69.95 (product number 12750) and requires no gunsmithing. The shooter simply unscrews the two bolts holding the halves of the mount together (using the L wrenches supplied by B-Square), places the unit on the frame, and tightens the two bolts. The mount is then ready to accept standard Weaver rings for scope attachment.

Once a shooter has a scope mount for his pistol, the next big decision is what type of scope to attach to it. Currently scopes fall into two broad categories, electric "dot" scopes and optical scopes.

Optical scopes with traditional crosshairs and no electronics to contend with have been on the scene a long time, though putting them onto a pistol has been a relatively modern occurrence. Most shooters find that 1-power magnification is generally best for handguns since it permits aiming with both eyes open, giving the illusion of a wider field of view since the shooters' eyes combine the two images coming into his brain. However some shooters, especially hunters, may want some magnification; in such a case, a 2x, 3x, or even 4x power scope might be a more suitable choice than a 1x-power scope.

Tasco's "Proclass" pistol scopes are good picks for handgunners wanting an optical scope. This line of scopes comes in a variety of powers and reticules. The scopes' 30mm tubes give longer eye relief and a greater field of view. The scopes are sold with 30mm rings so mating them to standard-sized Weaver mounts is simple.

Shooters of the tall persuasion considering the purchase of a cross-hair optical scope should always check for adequate eye relief (the distance from the eye to the scope) before they make any purchases; a few optical cross-hair scopes don't have long enough eye relief for those with longer arms. Also, it's a good idea to purchase a name brand scope like Bushnell, Tasco, or others to insure quality of the optics as well as simplified repair of the scope if it is ever damaged. Bargain scopes with little-known names are almost always iffy at best and a waste of money in the long run.

Dot scopes place a dot at the center of a scope's field of view, dispensing with cross hairs and the like. That said, it would seem that this wouldn't be a big advantage; and it wasn't — until manufacturers started "lighting" the dot. Then it became very easy for a shooter to find the glowing dot in his field of vision and, with practice, permitted quick acquisition of a target. This changed the whole idea of scopes for many shooters and is the reason dot scopes are seen on many competition guns.

There are two types of dot scopes: Those operating on available light and those functioning with a small battery to produce a glowing dot via an LED (Light-Emitting Diode). Of the two, the battery-operated version has become the most popular since the brightness of the dot can be adjusted according to the tastes of the shooter.

Many competition shooters employ guns sporting electric "dot" scopes. The advantage of this type of scope is that they permit aiming with both eyes open and have little if any parallax problems. They're just as tough as other optical scopes to bring onto the bull's eye, but shooters who practice extensively with these scopes can learn to rapidly acquire a target. If speed is a shooter's goal, then the dot scope coupled with lots of practice will deliver.

Dot scopes have another plus over cross-hair optical scopes. They can be used in the dark, producing a sight picture much like that of the laser — without giving away the shooter's presence to anyone in the target area since a dot scope, unlike a laser sight (more on these in a bit), produces no indication of its presence to the front of the pistol. Dot scopes thus work not only during the day but at dusk or even nighttime for those using the firearm in self defense.

Dot scopes also have unlimited eye relief and don't suffer from any parallax problems; this permits a target to be accurately hit without placing the dot in the center of the field of view in the scope picture, an important plus for quick target acquisition and shooting. Most dot scopes display a tiny (usually red but sometimes green) ball of light in the center of the scope "picture."

While electric scopes are quick in acquiring targets, they aren't quick to turn on. It's generally necessary to twist a knob or, more rarely, throw a switch. Unfortunately no enterprising manufacturer has yet marketed a pressure switch similar to those described below which are common to laser sights nor has anyone created a mercury switch that turns the scope on when the pistol is drawn from its holster.

For this reason electric scopes should be turned on the moment a shooter expects to be shooting—an especially important point for those using these scopes for hunting or self defense. (Fortunately battery life is very long for these scopes, making it possible to leave the scope on for extended time without fear of running down the battery—provided the battery is replaced on a regular basis.)

The best of the electric dot scopes currently available are offered by Aimpoint, AAL Optics, and Tasco. Tube size on the models offered by these companies varies; older 1-inch models are less expensive but give a narrower field of view than the newer 30mm or larger scopes do, making them less rapid in acquiring the target. Most shooters will discover they can acquire a target more rapidly if they purchase one of these larger scopes for their handgun.

In addition to costing less, the 1-inch tube scopes are also more compact. For those trying to carry a scoped gun in a holster, it makes a lot of sense to go with a 1-inch scope simply because it is smaller and therefore less apt to be bumped or damaged when being carried.

The Aimpoint 5000 offers a 30mm field of view. This scope is available in black matte or stainless finish, the scope can be powered by a pair of mercury SP675 batteries or, for cold weather use, a single lithium 2L76 or DL1/3N battery. The scope is 5.5 inches long and weighs 5.8 ounces; cost is $320. Since the 5000 scopes have tubes too large for one-inch Weaver rings, these are included with the scope and will accommodate most Weaver-style mounts.

Aimpoint's "Comp" scope is designed to capture a share of the competition shooting market. The 30mm field of view helps a shooter lock onto his target. Weight of the Comp scope is 4.75 ounces and the length is 4.365 inches. The scope comes with rings to permit easy mounting on Weaver rails.

Tasco's "ProPoint" series of electric dot scopes have either 30mm tubes (which give a 25mm field of view) or 40mm tubes (giving a 30mm field of view). These scopes come with mounting rings and detachable sun shields that screw onto the front and/or rear of the scope. The ProPoints come in three dot sizes (dot size is measured in minutes of angle with a minute covering a 1-inch area at 100 yards).

The Tasco Propoint PDP2 and PDP3 have 30mm tubes with a choice of 5- or 10-minute sized dots; the PDP2 has an on/off switch while the PDP3 has an 11 position rheostat for fine adjustment of dot brightness. The PDP4 has a 45mm tube and comes in three dot sizes of 10, 15, and 20 and has an 11-position detent. Costs vary according to models and the best deals offered by dealers, but the Propoint scopes generally sell in the $190 to $250 range.

AAL Optics offers a 30mm dot scope as their "Ultra Dot 30" which incorporates its battery pack into the small, click-adjustable brightness control knob, eliminating the cumbersome projecting battery pack seen on most other dot scope designs. The cost for the Ultra Dot 30 is $189; the scope is available in a choice of stainless and matte black finish.

The AAL dot scopes have always had the plus of being an ounce or so lighter than their competitors. Recently AAL has shaved off even more weight by switching to a tough injection molded composite tube (rather than aluminum) for the body of the "Ultra Dot Patriot" (the "Patriot" designation coming from the fact that it is one of the few dot scopes that's made entirely in the U. S.A). In addition to its light weight, this scope has a fiber optic system that makes its red dot sharper and rounder than the dot of some other scopes. Cost is also less; the scope retails for $119.

"Tubeless" dot scopes have appeared on the market. These have the advantage of permitting the shooter to see the red dot on the mirrored lens at the front of the scope since it lacks a tube to block the view. This makes for quicker target acquisition and also a lighter sight. Of course the downside is that the sight is open, making it somewhat more sensitive to dirt than a sealed scope system. For those using the scope for self defense, it should also be noted that the LED may be somewhat visible from the side on some of these units, a potential tactical problem in very dark surroundings.

The tubeless system is based on an early 1900s-vintage shotgun sight. This design was resurrected in the 1970s by Daisy Air Rifles as a cheap plastic scope for air guns. Later, this design was modified with the addition of an LED (Light-Emitting Diode) and small electric watch battery so it would work in all types of light rather than just bright sunlight.

Since the patent has expired on the original design, several manufacturers have created more expensive versions of the open sight with a larger lens and 1-inch Weaver mounts, rather than the smaller 7/8-inch mounts common to air rifles and .22 rifles. But except for the larger field of view and sealed battery packs, these more expensive open sights are quite similar to Daisy's.

Currently Emerging Technology offers an open dot scope as its "Dualdot" model in its LaserAim series of products. In addition to providing an optical dot, this scope has a laser sight built into its base which can be ideal for some night shooting situations. Cost of the Dualdot is $225.

Whether you choose an electric dot scope or an optical scope, it's important to put in extensive practice with it. This makes it possible to quickly bring the pistol onto its intended target without having to "hunt" around for it.

● ● ● ● ●

The Heckler & Koch pistols are hard to improve on, just as they come from the box. Thought and care should be given before altering any of these firearms, whether the change is a bolt-on accessory or a customized compensator. Accessories and modifications can't be substituted for the skill that comes with thoughtful practice. Expert shooters don't get that way because of the accessories they own or the modifications they've made to their pistols. Skilled shooters become good because they've spent many, many hours at the pistol range.

Practice does make perfect — or as close to perfect as is humanly possible on this side of heaven.

Heckler & Koch's Handguns

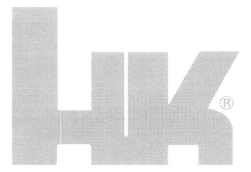

Chapter 4
Maintenance

All of the Heckler & Koch guns are noted for their reliability. But like any other firearm or machine, the pistols operate better if they're given proper maintenance. With care, reliability problems become almost nonexistent and wear will be less excessive as the gun ages and the number of rounds that have gone through it mount up.

Prime consideration must be given to proper lubrication between the various moving parts of the firearm; not just any lubricant will do the job. Oils designed for electrical engines or penetrating oils like WD40 are best avoided on firearms for two reasons. These lubricants often solidify over time when exposed to the air; creating binding that causes firearm malfunctions. Second, penetrating oil is more apt than regular gun oils to deactivate the cartridge in a firearm — not too handy a happenstance whether in contest shooting or in combat.

Oil must be very carefully applied with gas-operated guns like the P7 series. Lubricant in the gas system will quickly carbonize when exposed to burning powder, fouling the pistol so it fails to function properly.

Modern, all-purpose cleaning/lubricating solvents designed for firearms are good choices for the Heckler & Koch guns. Tri-Lube, Break-Free CLP, or one of the other formulas is perfect.

Heckler & Koch's Handguns

The shooter should *lightly* oil all moving parts, taking care not to get any lubricant on cartridges or leave excessive amounts where it might run onto cartridges. With most of the Heckler & Koch pistols, oil is only needed to prevent rust on blued surfaces. A quick check of the owner's manual will suggest whether the surface in question is blued or has an oxide or epoxy finish; the latter groups don't require oil to prevent rust. Nor does a plastic or nickel finish.

Stainless steel is not completely stainless. It is only rust resistant. That means a light coat of car wax or oil is helpful to prevent corrosion — especially in areas with salt spray or high humidity. Stainless steel surfaces that move against other bearing surfaces do need lubrication, contrary to what some shooters seem to think.

Excessive lubricant acts like a dust magnet, collecting grit that can become like tiny files on moving surfaces. Inordinate amounts of oil can also damage holsters and stain clothing. For this reason oil should be used in moderation and should not be applied on the exterior of a firearm unless it is necessary to prevent rust.

Another option for lubricating a Heckler & Koch pistol is the new "dry lube" developed by Brownells' and marketed as the "Action Magic II". While the idea of a "dry" lubrication based on silicon or graphite particles is hardly new, most of these products haven't proven overly reliable on firearms, due to the temperature extremes and bizarre environments that most guns are subjected to as well as the intense heat generated by the igniting of a cartridge in a pistol.

Action Magic II changes this situation since the lubricant has been formulated with a pistol shooter in mind. After the firearm has been thoroughly cleaned, two different applications are made to its moving parts with time needed for each to dry. Once dry, the lubricants in Action Magic II actually bond with the metal of the firearm and provide lubrication without any oil that will attract dust and dirt.

In addition to lubricants, Action Magic II contains rust inhibitors. This makes this lubricant ideal both for very dirty environments and also does away with any potential of the lubricant to deactivate cartridges. Action Magic II also helps with cleanup because its slick surface tends to repel dirt; often simply wiping a gun with a soft nylon brush is all the cleaning it will need, with the exception of the bore, though some shooters even place Action Magic II inside the bore of their firearm and claim that cleaning is equally quick in this area as well.

Action Magic II costs $16.75 from Brownells. The bottles the shooter gets for this amount will last for quite some time with careful use and the material is safe to use inside bores as well as on triggers, slide/frame interface, hammers, strikers, etc.

Cleaning a gun dictates field stripping if the job is to be done properly (more on disassembly steps in a moment). A barrel should never be cleaned from the muzzle end since this can damage the lands at the end of the barrel, ruining accuracy. Instead brushes and swabs should travel from the chamber toward the muzzle and then on out, not returning since that drags fouling back into the bore, defeating much of the work that's being done. As for the cleaning kit, a visit to a gunstore will turn up a variety of cleaning kits complete with brushes sized to fit the 9mm-, .40-, or .45-sized bore.

The first thing to do when cleaning the bore is to send a swab or the bore brush through the barrel after soaking the instrument to the point of dripping with liberal amounts of solvent. Then the barrel should be set aside for a half hour so the solvent can really break down the dirt in the barrel.

A cleaning brush soaked in solvent is then shoved down the bore to break up the last of the fouling deposits coating the inside of the barrel. If this chore is done regularly, then buildup from metal jackets will be easily removed, saving a lot of work in the long run and also avoiding the possibility of dangerous chamber pressures produced when the bore is "contracted" in size by excessive metal buildup inside it.

The shooter next runs cloth or paper towel swabs through the bore, again moving from the chamber to the muzzle. Some shooters prefer jags for this chore while others like the slotted cleaning tools. Either will do the job just fine and is more a matter of taste than utility.

At the end of the barrel cleaning job, the shooter sends a dry patch through the bore followed by a patch soaked in solvent. This alternating process continues until the patches start to come through clean.

If the gun is to be stored away, the operation ends with an oil-soaked patch going though the bore. If the gun is to be loaded, a dry patch is sent through last to keep the oil from ruining the accuracy of the first shot as well as to prevent the lubricant from deactivating the cartridge.

An inordinate number of firearms accidents occur because guns aren't unloaded *before* the cleaning process is started. Be sure to remove the magazine from a semiauto *first* and then cycle the slide and check the chamber to be sure the gun is empty before you start to clean it.

Even when you're sure a firearm is empty, it's wise to still point it in a safe direction at all times. If you get into the habit of doing this, then you'll be less apt to point a loaded gun at someone by mistake. And that, too, can prevent a lot of accidents.

Field Stripping the Heckler & Koch Pistols

Field stripping is all that's needed for basic maintenance of the Heckler & Koch pistols covered in this book. The pistols are generally easy to dismantle farther, but it's a good idea to avoid disassembling any firearm beyond field stripping unless such is necessary for repair or parts replacement. More modern guns are damaged through disassembly beyond field stripping than by actual use these days. Don't yield to the temptation to dismantle a pistol farther than is necessary to clean and care for it. Otherwise you may lose or damage the pistol.

Because of the major differences of design between the various Heckler & Koch pistols, field stripping is quite different from one model to the next.

Field Stripping the HK4

1) The magazine should first be removed and the firearm cycled and the chamber checked to be sure it's empty.

2) Cock the hammer and place the safety in the "safe" position.

3) The takedown latch in the front of the trigger guard is pushed down and forward to release the slide.

4) With the slide release held down, the slide is eased forward one fourth of an inch and lifted off the frame.

5) Turn the slide assembly upside down and push the barrel forward and point the chamber downward and ease it and the recoil spring surrounding it from the slide. Take care to retain the spring and barrel assembly as they are under pressure in the slide.

Reassembly is a reverse of this process.

Field Stripping the P7

1) Remove the magazine and cycle the firearm, checking the chamber to be sure it's empty.

2) While depressing the takedown latch at the left rear of the frame (just below the slide), ease the slide back one half inch and lift the slide upward off the frame. Take care to retain the slide assembly as it is under pressure from the recoil spring around the barrel.

Reassembly is a reverse of this process.

Field Stripping the P9/P9S

1) The magazine should first be removed and the firearm cycled and the chamber checked to be sure it's empty.

2) Push the takedown latch at the inside front of the trigger guard up and forward to release the slide.

4) With the slide release held up, the slide is eased forward one-half inch and lifted off the frame.

5) Turn the slide assembly upside down and push the barrel forward and point the chamber downward and ease it and the recoil spring surrounding it from the slide. Take care to retain the spring and barrel assembly as they are under pressure in the slide.

Reassembly is a reverse of this process.

Field Stripping the USP

1) The magazine should first be removed and the firearm cycled and the chamber checked to be sure it's empty.

2) The slide is retracted slightly (about 1/2 inch) and held back to line up the square recess on the left of the slide over the rod of the slide release. The rod of the release is then pushed from the right side of the frame while the slide is held back.

3) After the slide release has been removed, the slide is then eased forward until it is off the frame.

4) Turn the slide assembly upside down and the spring guide and recoil springs can be removed from the barrel.

5) The barrel can now be lifted out of the slide.

Reassembly is a reverse of this process.

Field Stripping the VP70

1) The magazine should first be removed and the firearm cycled and the chamber checked to be sure it's empty.

2) The slide is retracted slightly and pull the release catch at the rear of the trigger guard.

3) Lift the slide upward off its tracks and then ease the slide forward until it is off the frame. Take care as the slide is under spring pressure.

4) The recoil spring can be removed from the barrel.

Reassembly is a reverse of this process.

Disassembly of Magazines

Most Heckler & Koch and aftermarket magazines can be disassembled by shoving the base plate forward and off the magazine; often this base plate is held in place with an inner plate. This dictates using a small tool to push the inner plate upward. Usually there is a hole in the base plate to give access to the inner plate. (With the USP magazines, it is also necessary to pinch the magazine tabs inward when releasing the base plate.)

Once the base plate is removed, the spring, inner plate (if present), and magazine follower must be restrained since the magazine spring is under pressure. Great care is necessary to keep track of the follower and its spring since each part has a top, bottom, forward, and rear sides; inserting the follower or

Maintenance

spring into the magazine incorrectly during reassembly will lead to malfunctions.

The Heckler & Koch "Clinton" magazines have their capacity limited with a spacer. This spacer holds the base plate detents in slots cut in the side of the magazine, making attachment of a traditional base plate impossible and thereby limiting the magazine capacity. To disassemble these, the center stud in the base of the magazine is shoved into the magazine, freeing the base plate. Then the spacer, base plate, spring and follower can be removed.

Care should be exercised to keep the various parts of the magazine aligned properly during reassembly. To get the base plate and spacer back onto the magazine, the spacer is placed part way into the magazine and the tabs on the base plate squeezed inward so they can fit into the bottom of the magazine after the spacer. Once the parts are shoved into the magazine, the tabs lock into the side of the magazine and keep everything in place.

With Ram-Line magazines as well as others having a "constant force" or clock-coiled spring, the removal of the base plate gives access to the inside of the magazine but doesn't free the spring or follower. With such magazines it's generally best to use some type of spray cleaner and then take care to thoroughly dry out the magazine and its spring. Pains should be exercised not to employ solvent sprays that will damage the plastic follower or sprays having water (which will promote rust). Ram-Line magazines can usually be disassembled by pushing on the locking tab on an inner plate through a hole in the base plate.

Following the cleaning, a plastic magazine can be reassembled without adding any lubrication to it. With metal magazines, a very light coating of oil will aid in both the magazine's functioning as well as in rust prevention on blued steel surfaces. Excess oil must be wiped away if the magazine is to be used in the near future as lubricant can deactivate ammunition. Plastic magazines are self-lubricating and should never have oil or other lubricants placed on them, though the springs might need a light coat of oil to prevent rust in very humid parts of the world.

129

Heckler & Koch's Handguns

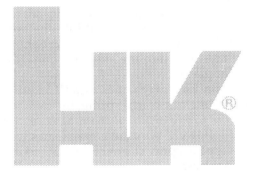

Appendix A
Accessories Sources

AAL Optics
2316 NE 8th Rd.
Ocala, FL 34470   904-629-3211

Aimpoint, USA
580 Herndon Parkway, Suite 500
Herndon, VA 22070   703-471-6828

B-Square Company
Box 11281
Ft. Worth, TX 76110   800-433-2909

Bausch & Lomb/Bushnell
9200 Cody
Overland Park, KS 66214 800-423-3537

Bianchi International, Inc.
100 Calle Cortez
Temecula, CA 92590   714-676-5621

Heckler and Koch's Handguns

Brigade Quartermasters
8025 Cobb International Blvd.
Kennesaw, GA 30144-4349   404-428-1248

Brownells, Inc.
Rt. 2, Box 1
Montezuma, IA 50171   515-623-5401

Choate Machine & Tool
Box 218
Bald Knob, AR 72010-0218 501-724-6193

Ed Brown Products
Rt. 2, Box 2922
Perry, MO 63462   314-565-3261

Heckler & Koch, GmbH
Box 1329
7238 Oberndorf/Neckar, Germany

Heckler & Koch, Inc.
21480 Pacific Blvd.
Sterling, VA 20166

Hesco, Inc.
2821 Greenville Rd.
LaGrange, GA 30240   404-884-7967

Hogue Grips
P.O. Box 2038
Apascadero, CA 93423   800-438-4747

Les Pitman Custom Gun Services
14765 Raritan Dr.
Whittier, CA 90604

Accessories Sources

Mag-na-port International
41302 Executive Dr.
Mt. Clemens, MI 48045-34488   313-469-6727

Michaels of Oregon Company
P. O. Box 13010
Portland, OR 97213   503-255-6890

Pachmayr
1875 S. Mountain Ave.
Monrovia, CA 91016   800-357-7771

Tasco Sports Optics
P.O. Box 520080
Miami, FL 33152-0080   305-591-3670

Heckler and Koch's Handguns

Appendix B
Useful Information

American Firearms Industry (Monthly magazine)
2455 E. Sunrise Blvd.
Ft. Lauderdale, FL 33304

American Rifleman (Monthly magazine)
National Rifle Association
1600 Rhode Island Ave., NW
Washington, DC 20036

Combat Handguns (Monthly magazine)
1115 Broadway
New York, NY 10010

Gun Digest (Yearly, book format)
DBI Books, Inc.
One Northfield Plaza
Northfield, IL 60093

Guns & Ammo (Monthly magazine)
P.O. Box 51214
Boulder, CO 80323-1214

SWAT (Monthly Magazine)
LFP, Inc.
9171 Wilshire Blvd., Suite 300
Beverly Hills, CA 90210

The following books are excellent sources of information about firearms, including the various Heckler & Koch guns:

The 100 Greatest Combat Pistols
By Timothy J. Mullin
Paladin Press
P. O. Box 1307
Boulder, CO 80306-1307

Cartridges of the World
By Frank C. Barnes
4092 Commercial Ave.
Northbrook, IL 60062

Combat Rifles of the 21st Century
By Duncan Long
Paladin Press
P. O. Box 1307
Boulder, CO 80306-1307

HK Assault Rifle Systems
By Duncan Long
Delta Press
P.O. Box 1625
215 S. Washington St.
El Dorado, AR 71731

Handgun Stopping Power
By Evan P Marshall and Edwin J. Sanow
Paladin Press
P. O. Box 1307
Boulder, CO 80306-1307

Useful Information

Laser Sights and Night Vision Devices
By Duncan Long
Delta Press
P.O. Box 1625
215 S. Washington St.
El Dorado, AR 71731

Military Small Arms of the 20th Century (6th Edition)
Ivan V. Hogg and John Weeks
4092 Commercial Ave.
Northbrook, IL 60062

Pistols of the World
By Ian V. Hogg and John Weeks
Presidio Press
1114 Irwin St.
San Rafael, CA 94901

The following videos are excellent sources of information about shooting techniques which can be applied to the Heckler & Koch pistols:

Basic Guide to Handguns
By Jeff Cooper
Mail Order Videos
7888 Ostrow St., Suite A.
San Diego, CA 92111

IPSC Secrets
By Brian Enos and Lenny Magill
Mail Order Videos
7888 Ostrow St., Suite A.
San Diego, CA 92111

Heckler & Koch's Handguns

Pistol Masters
By Rob Leatham (with Brian Enos, J. Michael Plaxco, and
  others)
Mail Order Videos
7888 Ostrow St., Suite A.
San Diego, CA 92111

Secrets of Gunfighting: Israeli Style
By Eugene Sockut
Paladin Press
P. O. Box 1307
Boulder, CO 80306-1307

Heckler & Koch's Handguns

	Self-loading Pistol **VP70 Z**
ЉК **Handguns**	 VP70Z

Calibre	9 mm x 19 (Luger)
Operating principle	recoil-operated
Bolt system	inertia bolt
Feed	18 round magazine
Mode of fire	single fire
Muzzle velocity -Vo-, approx.	1180 f.p.s. (360 m/s)
Muzzle energy -Eo-	376 ft.lbs. (520 J)
Sights	movable rear sight — shadow front sight
Weights	
Pistol without magazine	1.80 lbs. (0.82 kg)
Pistol with magazine, filled	2.51 lbs. (1.14 kg)
Pistol with holster stock, without magazine	—
Holster stock	—
Magazine, empty	3.50 oz. (100 g)
Cartridge	185 grs. (12 g)
Lengths	
Pistol	8.01 in. (204 mm)
Pistol with holster stock	—
Barrel	4.55 in. (116 mm)
Sight radius	6.90 in. (175 mm)
Width/height of pistol	1.26/5.60 in. (32/142 mm)

A 1970's lineup of the Heckler & Koch, Inc., pistol family.

140

Self-loading Pistol **VP70 M**	Self-loading Pistol **P7**
VP70M	P7
9 mm x 19 (Luger)	9 mm x 19 (Luger)
recoil-operated	recoil-operated
inertia bolt	retarded inertia bolt
18 round magazine	8 round magazine
single fire and 3 shot burst	single fire
1180 f.p.s. (360 m/s)	1150 f.p.s. — 1450 f.p.s. (350 — 425 m/s)
376 ft.lbs. (520 J)	340 — 405 ft.lbs. (460 — 550 J)
movable rear sight — shadow front sight	movable rear and front sight
1.80 lbs. (0.82 kg)	1.80 lbs. (0.82 kg)
2.51 lbs. (1.14 kg)	2.16 lbs. (0.98 kg)
2.82 lbs. (1.28 kg)	—
1.01 lbs. (0.46 kg)	—
3.50 oz. (100 g)	2.45 oz. (70 g)
185 grs. (12 g)	185 grs. (12 g)
8.01 in. (204 mm)	6.54 in. (166 mm)
21.40 in. (545 mm)	—
4.55 in. (116 mm)	4.13 in. (105 mm)
6.90 in. (175 mm)	5.79 in. (147 mm)
1.80/5.65 in. with holster stock (46/144 mm)	1.10/4.92 in. (28/125 mm)

Drawing courtesy of Heckler & Koch, Inc.

141

Heckler & Koch's Handguns

Self-loading Pistol **P9 S**	Self-loading Pistol **HK4**
P9S	HK4
9 mm x 19 (Luger) – .45 ACP	.380 ACP – .32 ACP – .25 ACP – .22LR (HV)
recoil-operated	recoil-operated
delayed roller-locked	inertia bolt
magazines for 9 or 7 rounds	magazines for 7 – 8 – 8 – 8 rounds
single fire	single fire
1148 f.p.s. – 853 f.p.s. (350 – 260 m/s)	950 – 820 – 787 – 820 f.p.s. (290 – 250 – 240 – 250 m/s)
361 – 364 ft.lbs. (500 – 504 J)	188 – 108 – 65 – 58 fts.lbs. (260 – 150 – 90 – 80 J)
square notch rear sight – movable post front sight	movable rear and front sight
1.87 lbs. – 1.74 lbs. (0.85 kg – 0.79 kg)	1.05 lbs. (0.48 kg)
2.26 – 2.22 lbs. (1.03 kg – 1.01 kg)	1.30 lbs. – 1.27 lbs. – 1.23 lbs. – 1.21 lbs. (0.59 kg – 0.58 kg – 0.56 kg – 0.55 kg)
–	–
–	–
2.62 oz. (75 g)	1.40 oz. (40 g)
185 grs. – 320 grs. (12 g – 20.8 g)	146 grs. – 117 grs. – 78 grs. – 52 grs. (9.5 g – 7.6 g – 5.1 g – 3.4 g)
7.55 in. (192 mm)	6.17 in. (157 mm)
–	–
4.00 in. (102 mm)	3.34 in. (85 mm)
5.77 in. (147 mm)	4.75 in. (121 mm)
1.33/5.55 in. (34/141 mm)	1.25/4.32 in. (32/110 mm)

Drawing courtesy of Heckler & Koch, Inc.

Notes

Notes

Notes

Other Books Available From Desert Publications